Table Of Contents

Chapter 1: What Is Digital Marketing?

Digital marketing is a term generally used for the marketing of services with the use of digital technology outlets. This is majorly on the internet, but it also consists of display advertising, mobile phones, and other digital channels.

Activities in digital marketing include the following:

- SEM (search engine marketing)
- campaign marketing
- influencer marketing
- SEO (search engine optimization)
- email direct marketing
- optical disks and games
- e-books
- e-commerce marketing
- display advertising and every other kind of digital media

It also covers all channels outside the internet that offer digital media. Some of these consist of mobile phones (MMS and SMS), ringtones played when on hold, and every other thing related.

What Are Digital Marketing Agencies

Industries in the digital marketing sector develop campaigns for advertisement; then these adverts are placed across digital media platforms. These agencies, in-house or subcontracting proficiencies, offer creative services, advice, and creation of materials for advertising, account management, and media purchasing and planning.

The digital marketing agency sector is quite a huge one. It is a field that is booming in all areas of the globe, especially in developed nations like Canada, Australia, Germany, the United Kingdom, and America.

The digital marketing industry will keep growing because many businesses are starting to see that, at some point, they will require a digital marketing agency to aid them in penetrating their target market and creating the brand awareness they need that will foster their expansion and growth. From the statistics available, we can safely presume that the sector is steadily rising even with the level of competition involved.

Entrepreneurs are urged to create digital marketing agencies of their own because it is affordable and easy to begin. You can begin one right from your home. All you have to do is establish an office in a part of your home. What individuals pay you for is the outcome you can provide them concerning their publicity and marketing issues.

How Does Digital Marketing Differ from Traditional Marketing?

In comparison to other traditional media that is usually too pricey, digital marketing does not need a huge budget. This is the reason organizations utilize new technology alongside platforms like Twitter, Instagram, YouTube, and Facebook among others to get to a broader target market. This is as opposed to using other tools for marketing, which can be pricey.

Now, digital marketing has become a crucial tool for the promotion of businesses as it has to do with services and products globally, not only to make sales to clients but also to keep them engaged. It is less complicated for organizations to broaden their market with the least capital investment.

How to Begin Your Digital Marketing Agency Business from Home

Here, we are going to cover how to begin your digital marketing agency. You will learn a few steps to help you begin.

First, let's take a look at some of the basics.

The first areas you need to focus on are your *platform* and your *foundation*—you need these to begin a digital agency and attain success along the way. These are the areas you hardly look at. However, if you do focus on these easy aspects, it can aid in saving you a lot of hassle moving forward.

Now, let's take a look at the first step here:

Be Optimistic

The first thing you need to understand is that there is no easy route to success. You won't just create an agency and succeed overnight. You will require determination, hard work, and many late nights.

However, in all, you will need a positive attitude to go through it. If you are beginning an agency, you need to have an image of what you desire to attain. Then you will need to hold on to that image in your mind for as long as you can.

Remember, do not get frustrated as your breakthrough could be just after your next rejection. Now that we have covered this, let us move on to the next step.

Establish Clear Goals

For you to attain success, you will require clear goals you plan on achieving. If you have no goal, it may be difficult to achieve something.

You may have various goals for wanting to begin an agency; however, like many others, one of your goals is to make money. This does not mean your goal cannot consist of other things that help you go forward.

View your goals as something you can attain. When you establish a target for yourself, you will be able to achieve it.

However, the best way to set your goal is to use SMART. Even though this may not seem original, it is quite functional. Now, a SMART goal should be something like this:

- Specific: Be precise about what you aim to achieve. Instead of something like, "I want to be a leader in the industry," you can instead say, "I want to generate $10,000 from sales during the first two years."

- Measurable: Here, you will provide an answer to the question "How will I know when I have attained my goal?"

- Achievable: What do you believe you can achieve within a specific period?

- Realistic: You need to understand that when setting up a goal, it has to be realistic. It is unrealistic to say you will land $2,000,000 in the first six months of work. This is probably impossible. However, over six years? Well, why not?

- Time-bound: You need to set a specific and clear time frame to attain your goal. It could be medium, short, or long term. All these are dependent on the goal you have in place.

In essence, if you plan on beginning a digital marketing agency now, your SMART goals could be as follows:

- Increase the members of my team to 20 by the first year.

- Have a client retainer of $300,000 in the first two years.

Although presently, you may not know what your specific goals are, it is crucial to take some time and determine it. Doing this will ensure you have a higher level of direction and focus, and this will also ensure that you remain optimistic even when the going gets tough.

Locate Your Focus

Having a goal will let you understand where to focus your energy and time. However, the focus here has to do with the people you are going to channel these efforts and time toward. This is the phase you get to understand your audience, what they are interested in, and who they are.

Leading brands offer a precise set of ideas to specific groups of individuals. Your job is to determine who these group of individuals are. When you begin, the urge to try and satisfy all individuals may be strong. This is because you want to quickly get those clients and fill your account with cash as quickly as possible. It is quite usual to have this feeling, and you don't need to bother about it. However, what you need to do is overcome this urge.

To make it easier, you need to make efforts to put these into consideration to get yourself more focused. It will also aid you in clarifying what you are making efforts to develop and those you are developing it for.

What is your niche? Who are the individuals you plan on working with and why do you want to? Are you targeting the food industry, small businesses, or large organizations? Understanding this can also aid you in narrowing the areas you search for contracts. Below are a few areas you can specialize in. They include the following:

- search engine optimization (SEO)
- sponsorship advertising
- directories
- rich media advertising
- classifieds
- video advertising
- email
- mobile messaging
- social media management
- digital display advertising
- lead generation
- mobile advertising
- banner advertising

Who are the individuals you want to draw in? Are you after tech experts, business professionals, or the newcomers in the field? This will aid you in locating the individuals you will identify with and how you will start developing a well-known brand.

What makes you stand out? There are numerous agencies already in existence, so how is yours going to be unique from the others? What areas do you care about or value that others do not?

Evaluating who you are and the value you are offering to clients is a crucial step in creating a profitable brand. You need to learn the art of rejecting those things that do not go with your goals, and you will attain success faster.

Develop Relationships

The relationships you develop and nurture even before you have to use them are very crucial. If you desire to begin a digital agency, you will have to reach out to individuals and offer value and assistance.

Perhaps you see an organization with a poor ranking or with a search term they should not be using. Or maybe you come across someone asking a question on a forum which you know the response to. All these can be a means of offering assistance, offering value, and getting ahead.

These conversations are your methods of developing leads. They can also be how you set a meeting up with the marketing department of a business and the way you develop your business into a profitable one.

Picture an image of all the organizations you would love to work with and the places your target audience spends the majority of their time. Search for those you would love to do business with. Put each of them on a list and contact them.

Your goal should not be to sell to them immediately. All you need to do is look for methods of offering value or creating connections with them.

Establish a Clear Identity for Your Brand

Your brand identity has to be clear for a host of reasons. Many people buy from those they like, and this is what numerous organizations are aware of.

However, there is a fact lots of individuals tend to ignore, which is very crucial—something that keeps them tied up as a whole. According to an article in Forbes, "A brand is a promise."

A brand is a promise to provide services that individuals can rely on—one that they love and can associate with, one that they are aware will offer them solutions every time without fail. Some people will hate your brand, and some will love it.

When creating a great brand, you have to determine the following:

- What is your promise? What do your audience and you find valuable? What does your brand signify? Go with one and focus on it.

- What is the voice of your brand? This is very crucial, especially for digital agencies. What group of individuals finds your voice appealing? The way you speak to an already established organization differs from how you speak to a start-up. You need to determine who you will be speaking to and the way you want to talk to them.

When you have sorted this out, you have a place to begin developing your slogan, logo, and other areas that will make a tangible brand.

Be Innovative

If you plan on being successful as a digital agency, taking risks has to be a part of you. Don't be scared of changing and overhauling things in your niche.

The same is also applicable when you want to run an idea that scares you. You might have an idea or pitch that you love, but you are worried your client won't find appealing. These are the ones that usually attain the most success and leave the most impression on individuals.

As opposed to trying to merge with the environment and copying what other agencies do, search for unique and innovative methods. Pick what they have done and improve it. Better still, you can spin it entirely and make something of yours.

There are lots of individuals who will find your ideas amazing and will love what you are aiming to achieve. When you have the appropriate goals and focus, it won't be an issue for you to locate them.

Kick-Starting the Business

Now that you understand the basics of beginning a digital marketing agency, what you need to do now is to transform this fantastic idea into a reality. All these steps are going to require time; however, they will be the foundation of your new agency.

Let us move on to learn what they are.

Go Online

You are going to be involved with internet marketing, and you should already understand that you will require a website to start getting revenue. However, it is not compulsory that you dig a hole in your pocket.

Most times, the first thing that comes to your mind when thinking about a website is the way it looks. Is the design appealing enough? Are my images the right size? These come to mind because you presume the design is crucial. It is for this reason even a website built with a straightforward template can cost you a lot of cash.

The vital realization that will help save you lots of cash is that functionality should be your priority. Some of the leading websites have a very simple design, but they draw in lots of revenue because of their ease of usage and simplicity.

When you are just beginning, what you need to do is get an edge on the basics. These include your branding and domain. When you sort these out, you can bother about the design at a later time. Numerous agencies have begun using a free theme on WordPress and grown to be successful in their respective niches. You can equally be one of them.

Develop a Great Portfolio

Actions have a more resounding effect than words. This is the reason why you need a result-driven and strong portfolio if you plan on attaining new businesses.

People will tend to buy from you if they see that you have worked with and provided solutions for a brand they recognize and trust. Because if they are able to trust you to do their work, then what is stopping them?

If you have no portfolio at the moment, you can easily solve it. Make efforts to do some work for people at a low price or even free of charge. You can equally develop some great relationships during the process. To easily do this, you can put together a list of past projects that your staff has completed previously as a placeholder till you can complete some agency-related jobs.

Having a portfolio is the least requirement an agency must possess. That is why it is crucial for you to have one available. A great portfolio includes the following:

- headlines and brief snippets

- comprehensive case studies showing results

- client's testimonials

- future targets and objectives for that client

Your portfolio should let people know that, aside from providing the outcomes they desire, you will continuously keep delivering these results to others.

Determine if the Additional Capital Is Necessary

When you begin a digital agency, you may feel that it costs a lot. You may think that it requires lots of investors and a ton of cash already saved if you want everything to start smoothly. However, if you know your way around it, you may not need to spend so much when starting your digital agency.

Lots of agencies started with a low amount of capital, and others started with one person. All these ended up as agencies worth millions. A perfect example of this is Nifty Marketing set up by Mike Ramsey.

The way to go about it is to understand the crucial things for you as a new company and those that are not. For instance, you don't have to purchase every SEO tool you can find. The costs from all these tools, some of which you may never even use, can dig a deep hole in your capital and running cost. Instead, pick the best tools from the list that will suit your needs.

Another way to cut cost is not buying that large office you don't need. If you are starting up with two employees, don't rent out an office space that will take ten employees in anticipation for when you grow. You may only rack up costs, and your growth may not come until later. Instead, pick a location that is adequate for the number of available staff presently. Later on, as you expand, you can equally move to a larger location.

Lastly, the more people invest in your agency, the more they remove from what is yours. It's best to go by yourself and attain the success you desire even if it takes a long time. The reward is worth it in the end.

Look for Cheaper Alternatives

Lots of things are required when you start your agency. Some of these include the following:

- advertising and awareness
- marketing
- locating clients
- offering customer service

Looking at all these necessities, you may start to feel like it is going to cost you a ton of cash to get them all going. However, this is not the case. If you know where to look, you can easily do all this at an affordable rate.

Instead of hiring staff who will come to sit in your office physically, you can go through websites like Fiverr and Upwork and develop a customer service team that will cost you $5 to $10 an hour.

As for marketing, look for methods of developing your word of mouth. This is still the best method of marketing, and it will cost you nothing and bring you huge business going forward.

Determine When Employees Are Crucial

Irrespective of how you feel about it, there will come a time when you will require extra hands. As your business grows bigger, you will not be able to do everything by yourself.

To ensure that your business goes beyond just hiring a certain number of employees, you have to scale when and how you hire them. Depending on your agency and the kinds of services you provide, the steps here may vary. However, to go past this transition, you need to take a look at the following steps:

Independently: Begin as a one-person business, and do as much as you can.

- **Freelancers:** When you have nurtured the business enough, make efforts to outsource jobs to freelance SEO specialists. These could be entire projects you allocate to them and take a percentage, or it could be parts of a project you split between them and yourself.

- **Part-time employee:** You can look for people around. You can start getting the services of a freelancer. Place someone on a contract for a specific number of tasks each week. By doing this, you will begin to understand how to pay salaries without having lots of overheads.

- **Full-time employee:** When you have started to make adequate cash, you can bring in a full-time employee to minimize your work. This will also let you bring in more clients because you now have the extra hands.

You can stop here, but if you want to grow larger, you will realize there is a moment you will need to hire more employees.

Just like all aspects of SEO, the right time and accuracy are crucial here. Don't begin with employees from the first day, and ensure you don't take too much time before bringing in extra hands.

Develop Your Knowledge of SEO

Becoming an expert in SEO is not a necessity when starting a digital agency. This is because you can always build up your experience as you go forward. SEO is continuously evolving and changing. Even the smallest change from Google can make even the most experienced user a newbie once more.

Ensure you learn the basics of SEO and the impact of any decision you make. Then you will have the capacity to learn the remainder as you move forward.

Learn Methods to Break It Down to Clients

Clients are not bothered about SEO. What they want to see are results, ROI, traffic, cash flow, and increasing their number of customers.

However, they care about knowing the steps you are taking and how they can benefit from it in the easiest way possible. So you need to look for ways of explaining what you are doing or plan to do and how it is going to benefit them.

Use language that they understand with ease. Doing this will make sure they can easily process all you are doing. You need to look for a way to do this that goes with the client you are working with and your brand. However, emphasizing on visuals and the benefits they stand to gain can do no wrong.

Become Social

You need to have social media platforms ready. These platforms can help in many ways.

- **Marketing:** It is spread by word of mouth, is easy to use, and won't cost you anything. You may share videos, posts, and other materials to draw people to your direction.

- **Generating new leads:** It may not seem like the best strategy for getting new clients, but it is a top strategy nonetheless. When you have a strong presence on social media, it enhances your possibility of getting new clients as well.

- **Customer engagement:** You will be able to sort out queries and see what others have to say about your brand and service. Moreover, your brand becomes more human to people who find you online.

However, you don't need to bother about using all the platforms on social media. Channel your energy to one or two. This way, you will be more focused, leading to more engagement, leads, and traffic from a very great profile as opposed to two mediocre ones.

Ensure All Your Creations Are Optimized

You need to ensure any page you create is properly optimized so that people will easily find you on search engines. This should be the case even if you are writing a guest post, creating videos, making a page on Twitter or any other thing.

Determine what you desire your rankings to be for and ensure you incorporate it into any content you create. Even if it's something that brings in a few leads or views monthly, it's better than nothing.

Determine Your Prices

Pricing shows your clients the value you give yourself. Your pricing should be based on what you feel your services are worth. You don't need to be bothered about what people will say about your prices, so long as you understand the value you will be offering them.

Any client who can tell the value of your services will find you irrespective of the price.

Put Together Tools for Reporting

Many clients may not have an interest in the technical aspects of your practice. Nonetheless, it is your job as a digital marketing agency to offer clients reports of your activities and the outcomes you are achieving. You also have to monitor these internally.

A tool like Microsoft Excel is a great starting point. You can alter it to suit your brand and save all your files permanently. Another great option is to use Google Docs, which automatically saves your data on Google Drive. However, it is not easy to remain organized here.

Learn Bookkeeping

To do this, you don't have to be an accountant. However, you need to track your earnings and where all your funds go. There are lots of invoicing software packages to take advantage of, but just keeping an easy spreadsheet of what comes and goes out of your agency monthly can be a great step in helping you keep track of all your cash at every moment.

Forecast

This is also a very crucial step. Visualizing the way your business will grow in the coming year, how it will look when it grows, and the way you want it to grow are significant parts of your success.

You will deal with great times, and there will also be tedious moments. Knowing when all these will take place is crucial to helping you manage your finances and time.

Chapter 2: How to Outsource the Entire SEO Process

SEO can also be called search engine optimization. It has to do with enhancing your brand's exposure as well as the amount and quality of site traffic via organic or non-paid search engine results.

SEO has a lot to do with people and understanding the things they search for on the web, the words they are utilizing, the solutions they seek, and the kind of content they want. When you know the answers to these questions, you will be able to create connections with individuals who are in search of the solutions you provide online.

Understanding the intention of your audience is one aspect of SEO, and providing it in a method that is easy for search engine crawlers to locate and understand is another aspect.

The Key Parts of SEO

SEO contains some key aspects which include the following:

Keywords

Previously, keywords were the only fundamental techniques in SEO. Now, even though they are still crucial, it is vital that they are selected with care. You have to research them properly and incorporate them into your content wisely so that they will have the effect you desire.

Keywords are phrases and words that your targets utilize in locating content online. Brands can also use these keywords in connecting with targets who are in search of their services and products. You can utilize keywords in optimizing your URLs and titles among others.

Content

This is another crucial aspect of SEO because it is what helps you get to your audience and engage them. For example, if you run an agency and need to enhance your reach and visibility, you can publish a range of blogs that have to do with choosing the right digital marketing agency. State the reason why your agency is the right one, the services you offer, and the benefits among many others.

When an individual looking for a digital marketing agency runs a search for this information, your blog will show up in the results, and from there, you will be able to develop a relationship with that potential client because you have offered significant information. If at any moment the prospect is ready to choose a digital marketing agency for his or her needs, your agency will be one of the first to come to mind.

When you create content, it needs to be relevant, informational, educational, sharable, and engaging. Content comes in a lot of forms, which include the following:

- web page content
- infographics
- podcasts
- social media posts
- blogs
- videos
- e-books and whitepapers

Off-Page SEO

Off-page SEO has to do with optimization practices that do not take place on the website of your agency. The major strategy utilized for this is the building of backlinks. This is because when you build backlinks from other reputable websites to yours, it will inform search engines that your site is valuable and of high quality. This can help in building your authority.

Local SEO

The importance of local SEO is on the rise as an increasing number of individuals utilize mobile devices for searching. Now, 57% of every search takes place on smartphones and tablets, and most of these searches have local intent (Sterling, 2017).

If you run an agency, for example, local SEO will make sure that when individuals close to you went searching for the top digital marketing agencies in town, your site will come up in the results. Aside from local keywords, some best SEO practices include adding your business to Google My Business, Google Maps, and claiming directory listings among many others.

Search Engine Marketing

Search engine marketing (SEM) has to do with the marketing efforts you pay for. It also consists of things like pay-per-click, social media ads, display ads, Google AdWords, and many others.

SEM usually is not a core aspect of an elaborate SEO strategy; however, it is useful because it can aid you in reaching highly targeted and new audiences.

Why Is SEO Important to Your Digital Marketing Agency?

SEO is vital to your digital marketing agency or any business for a host of reasons, which include the following:

It Enhances Your Rankings and Visibility

This is one of the most crucial SEO functions. It can aid in enhancing your visibility, which would mean that prospects will not have a hard time finding your agency when they look for a solution you are providing. Visibility has a direct relationship to how you rank.

If your ranking is high on a search engine result page (SERP), prospects are more likely going to find your website and click. If your SEO labors are productive, your ranking and visibility will be higher. This is very crucial because the majority of those who search for a solution on the internet do not go past the first page.

It Increases in Web Traffic

This is one of the core objectives of SEO, and your traffic increases when your rankings and visibility do. Think about this for a bit: Almost 33% of clicks take place on the rankings on the first page. Additionally, more than 75% of every click goes to the initial five listings (Lee et al., 2013).

If you desire your agency website to be found by more prospects via a search engine, then you need SEO practices that will aid you in ranking in one of the top three positions, or better still, number one.

It Increases the Authority of your Website

Authority is becoming crucial to a search engine because its importance among users is on the rise. Authority connotes that your website is relevant, of high quality, trustworthy, and has something valuable to provide.

The higher the authority of your website, the higher the ranking your website will have, and the more trust prospects will have for your brand.

It Creates an Enhanced Visitor Experience

SEO is also vital because all the efforts and time you channel into producing fantastic content and ensuring your website is optimized with on-page SEO enhances your website's usability, and this develops a positive and seamless customer experience. For example, when you make your website more responsive, it will be easy for desktop or laptop, or mobile visitors to use. Also, by enhancing the load speed of your page, you will minimize your bounce rate and urge visitors to spend more time on your website. Almost 50% of visitors anticipate that a page loads in two seconds, and the more time it takes to load, the more your bounce rate and the less your conversions.

It Helps with Growth

SEO is crucial because it can aid your agency in achieving lots of its goal. It gives you an upper hand over your competition and boosts conversions that can result in more loyal clients, sales, and additional development for your organization.

It Has an Impact on the Buying Cycle

Clients always research before making a purchase. This is one of the main benefits of the Web from the point of view of the buyers. By using SEO strategies to pass your message for great deals, innovative services or products can make a huge difference in your sales.

If you do it right, it will undoubtedly affect your buying cycle the right way.

You Can Use It for a Long Time

You will be able to see the effect of the SEO steps you are taking during the first year. Also, lots of these steps will have an effect that lasts over numerous years. And the higher the budget, time, and effort you commit on your SEO, the longer a website will have the capacity to be a major competitor in its market.

SEO Helps in Opening Up New Opportunities

High-quality SEO will always find a way of helping brands pinpoint and leverage new opportunities that will help them not just be found but also be successful. The better people understand a brand, the more the opportunities that will come up to ensure it excels. You can say the same thing about SEO.

What's the Best Way to Outsource Your SEO?

You understand the importance of SEO, and you also know that it is essential for you to channel some of your focus toward it. However, coupled with other activities like the administration of your business and getting more clients, time is not enough. Now that you understand that it is impossible for you to take on everything by yourself, you may be considering outsourcing SEO but don't know where to begin.

The great news is that there are numerous routes you can take when you want to outsource your SEO, but you need to make your choice with caution. You can choose to go with a freelancer or an SEO contractor.

It may be a difficult choice to make, but we will be covering all the options at your disposal as well as the benefits and drawbacks of outsourcing your SEO jobs to them.

SEO Freelancers

You can find SEO freelancers on websites like Fiverr or Upwork. They can also reliably carry out your tasks at a low price. The benefit of working with freelancers is that they already know what to do, and you don't need to spend time learning how to execute SEO tactics.

If the needs of your agency are minimal, freelancers are the ideal choice for you. It will also give you the capacity to choose freelancers when it is convenient for you and let you save cash in the process.

However, the downside to this is that the industry for internet marketing changes at a fast pace, and it can be a job on its own to follow the upcoming updates and trends. If you pick a freelancer that is not abreast with the current SEO requirements and trends, you will get obsolete work. Also, lots of websites require extensive SEO work, so you may add up cost faster if you go with a freelancer.

SEO Contractors

The benefits you get from hiring an SEO contractor is almost the same as what you get from a freelancer. Contractors can aid you in performing very technical and accurate SEO work, but you need to understand that a contractor is one individual. If you go with a contractor that has more than one client, which is always the case if he or she is excellent at their job, you will see yourself spending more time to get tasks done.

SEO Company

The benefit of going with this option is that you are not working with one person but a company. So aside from the fact that you won't have to spend time teaching yourself SEO, executing techniques you have picked up, and following the changing industry trend, you will also be working with a team of SEO experts.

SEO companies often comprise of a team of experts working alongside each other in the digital marketing sector daily. They often inform one another of new strategies and ideas. In essence, your business and campaign will undoubtedly enjoy the combined knowledge and experience a group has to offer.

The drawback of a company, however, is that there may be a limitation in the type of service they can offer you. If you need to carry out a task that has nothing to do with SEO, you may have to look for another agency.

Full-Service Agency

Similar to the above, you will be working in collaboration with a team of experts, but this team will be skilled enough to help with all your digital marketing requirements with one meeting, email or call.

You may have a single major point of contact when working with this agency. This individual will aid in managing your account and coordinating all the services you need. This will let you execute any digital marketing approach you need to achieve your marketing goals successfully.

When you outsource your SEO to this form of agency, it means you will work regularly and closely with the agency. Your point of contact in the agency will get to be a comprehensive part of your company, which can help you take off a lot of workloads. Aside from avoiding any back and forth when you need to get something done, your marketing tasks will go faster as well.

Also, when you work with a full-service agency, you will enjoy working alongside a team consisting of digital marketing experts and not just experts in SEO. This agency will have social media marketers, copywriters, and many others with vast experience you can exploit.

This sort of agency can be of great value to you in the long run. If you have an issue, there is a high possibility that someone in the agency has already faced it and come up with a solution before, which means any issue you throw their way can be sorted fast and accurately.

Why Do You Need to Outsource SEO?

SEO is very crucial for businesses. However, it is complex and takes a lot of time. Worse still, it gets complex each day. Do you run your own business, or are you involved in marketing and don't have adequate time to learn the trades and tricks of SEO and execute them? If your answer to this is yes, then outsourcing SEO is ideal for you.

Advantages of Outsourcing SEO

By outsourcing your SEO process, you stand to gain a lot of benefits. This is the case especially if you do not have adequate resources to oversee the entire process effectively.

Below are a few of the benefits that come with outsourcing:

Time to Focus on Other Essential Tasks

By outsourcing your SEO process to a reliable and trustworthy partner, you will be able to channel your energy to other crucial business areas.

You will be able to focus on attaining new clients for your agency and developing great client relationships.

On-Demand Services

When you outsource to providers of SEO services, you don't need any subscription plan. What you require is what you pay for when you require. Because of this, your overhead costs are less, but the revenue is higher.

Access to Experts

By outsourcing your SEO to an experienced service provider, you won't need to bother about hiring or training new staff. You won't even need to bother with creating new strategies. This is because you will be working with a team of SEO specialists who will be working on your needs. You will also be privy to tested and tried SEO techniques.

Hiring a Full-Time SEO Expert Is Pricey

It can be quite costly to hire a professional SEO expert full-time for your agency. In the United States, the average salary is $63,188 yearly.[4] In the UK, it is around £24,982 every year.[5] It can be a considerable burden on you especially as a startup agency to pay them salaries each month. You will also need to provide employment benefits, all of which can be a huge burden on you and your business.

When you outsource your SEO to experienced third parties, you will be saving a tremendous amount of cash.

It Offers Scalable Outcomes

You may hire an employee for your SEO requirements who can bring you 20 excellent links monthly. However, what if your need surpasses that? What if you need 200? The employee may be unable to achieve this figure.

SEO experts have processes that have been tried and tested over the years to locate opportunities for building links, developing content, and other things. They can provide you with scalable results when and how you require them. What this means is that they can expand and contract what they offer, depending on the need.

SEO Is Complex and Vital

SEO is very vital if you aim to be successful in digital marketing. Moreover, it is quite complicated. When ranking a site in its SERPs, Google considers over 200 factors. This can be a massive number to keep in mind, especially if you are not experienced in the field. Why not outsource this job to professionals who do it for a living?

Purchasing SEO Tools Is Not Necessary

SEO tools like SEMrush can be quite pricey, especially if you are just starting your digital marketing agency. An annual subscription for the pro version of SEMrush costs $99.95 monthly. If you are doing the SEO by yourself, such costs have to be on you. On the other hand, if you are outsourcing your SEO, the provider will have a subscription in place, and you won't have to spend so much on purchasing them.

Drawbacks of SEO Outsourcing

As the owner of an agency or business with a website, you have to weigh in the benefits as well as drawbacks. Below are some of the drawbacks of outsourcing your SEO needs.

Compromise in Quality

In a bid to minimize cost, there may often be a compromise in the quality of service rendered. Cheaper is not always the best. Ensure that you are getting the quality you desire for the amount you are paying for the service.

Distance

Most times, when you outsource, it is to someone or a company far away from your location. This means there will be a vast distance between you both, and communication will be via calls and emails among others. This sort of distance can result in communication issues along the line.

Doubts

When you hire a company not close to you or in another country entirely, it can be a huge risk, unless you have worked with them previously. Additionally, companies offering the same thing can offer diverse results. This means you cannot evaluate a company until you begin doing business with them.

Cultural Differences

Because of globalization, working across boundaries has become less difficult; however, there may still be existing cultural barriers that may affect the task at hand. Differences in holidays and festivals may result in some delay in completing tasks from both parties.

How to Outsource SEO

Now that we have covered the benefits of outsourcing your SEO and the options you have when you want to outsource, let us take a look at how to outsource your SEO correctly to ensure you get the results you desire.

Locate a Reputable SEO Company

The company or individual you outsource your SEO campaign or process to has a lot of influence on how successful it will become. If your choice is a good one, then you are probably going to get some fantastic results.

However, making the wrong choice can result in you wasting funds and depending on the strategies utilized by the person or firm you hired. You can equally have a penalty to deal with as well.

When in search of a freelancer or SEO firm to outsource the SEO needs of your agency, do not search for one offering the cheapest. Also, avoid companies that make you mouth-watering promises even before having a look at your website.

Don't just take in everything they tell you. Instead, request that they show you a sample of work they have previously done. Also, you can request that they create a proposal personalized to your specific requirements.

Look beyond SEO

SEO has to do with more than SEO. When you are talking about SEO, it means you are outsourcing the presence of your organization on the internet.

This implies that the services you are provided with should go beyond SEO. It is only an aspect of what you can do in an appropriate internet marketing campaign.

The firm you are outsourcing to should have the capacity to manage your email marketing, PPC campaigns, social media, and other things. They should also be able to tell you how all these can aid in growing your business.

These are the activities that will ensure that you get great ROIs when you outsource your SEO.

Develop Measurable Targets

Before you pay any money or sign any contract, you need to have some form of agreement with the firm that will aid in executing the project for what they will deliver.

When the project ends, what are they going to deliver? Are they going to deliver reports consisting of a list of more traffic, actions, and followers on

Facebook? Is it higher rankings on Google?

Don't set targets you can't measure. A great benefit of the internet is that you can measure everything. This means an SEO task can have measurable and specific targets.

Decide on an Action Plan

A great SEO campaign can take many months, and it is not a process that takes one month or a week. So using this duration, you need to create a comprehensive plan with intermediate targets and milestones. What are the actions you need to execute every month and what are the results you expect?

An excellent method of knowing the precise actions required is to request that the firm carries out an SEO audit of your website before the project begins. This will cost you a one-time fee, but the audit result will consist of action plans that you can translate into a project plan.

Track the Progress

Tracking progress in an SEO process is crucial, similar to other kinds of projects. You don't want to continue spending cash when you do not see any measurable results. Also, you don't want to continue paying for more than the months required to finish up a project.

The least difficult and leading way of monitoring whoever you outsource your SEO is to request for a comprehensive report monthly. In the report, the firm or individual needs to state the precise actions they take in a month, alongside the improvement as regards social media, terms of traffic, and user engagement among others.

Begin with a Small Budget

When you decide to outsource a process, you should have a budget in mind. What you need to be aware of when outsourcing your SEO process is that the results you seek may require a few months and may sometimes take years.

So if your agency is dependent on the internet, it is best to reduce the monthly budget and extend it over a few months. For instance, if you have a budget of $20,000, you can get into an agreement to spend $500 each month for 40 months as opposed to spending $5,000 for four months.

This is dependent on a host of other factors, and that is why you have to cover this comprehensively with your SEO organization before you sign any contract.

Develop SEO Skills In-house

There are SEO processes that require in-depth knowledge and expertise. However, there are aspects that people without SEO experience can efficiently execute.

Depending on your staff availability and the budget you have set aside for outsourcing SEO, you can decide to develop some skills in-house for the easy tasks and invest your money on outsourcing processes that can only be handled by a seasoned SEO professional.

The best method of dealing with this is by discussing it with your SEO company or expert. They should have the capacity to point out the tasks you can do in-house and offer the training needed as well.

Questions to Ask an SEO Provider before Working with Them

The following are a few questions or things to look out for before using the services of an SEO provider.

Available Services

Take a look at the list of services they can provide for campaigns. What kind of SEO task do they include? What is the amount of content they will offer?

Be sure of all the services they provide as these will help you get the most value for any cash you invest.

What SEO Tools Do They Use?

Ask your SEO company the tools they use. There are great SEO tools like SEMRush and BuzzSumo. If they mention any of these legitimate tools, then you can work with them. However, there are equally shady tools on the market that providers utilize for black hat SEO strategies. If the provider you have in mind begins to mention names like The Best Spinner among others, it is best to find someone else.

Employee Experience

Find out the individuals who will be handling your SEO processes. What are their qualifications or experiences? It is crucial that you find the appropriate individuals to help you with the job. Speak to them about your SEO needs. Your interaction with them will help you understand how capable they are.

What Are the Kind of Reports They Send?

Ask the SEO firm or provider you want to go with the kind of reports they will be sending your way. You will require a report that you can understand with ease. A standard SEO report should consist of on-page SEO analysis, website audits, alongside recommendations you should implement.

Gauging SEO Effectiveness

The SEO firm or specialist you are planning on going with should have the capacity to break down the metrics that they will utilize in measuring how effective their SEO efforts are. You should be provided access to their dashboard, which will monitor the performance of your processes and display your keyword rankings.

Have They Had Past Success?

If the provider has no previous success story to show you, it's best to find someone else. A great firm will take you through previous case studies and share the results they have had in the past. This will act as evidence of their previous success.

Red Flags to Note

When trying to pick an SEO firm, there are some red flags to look out for before you outsource your SEO process. If you notice any of these things in the company or freelancer you are about to go with, then it is best to walk away.

Not Going with the Guidelines of Google

An SEO expert that does not follow the guidelines put down by Google is certainly not a great one. This is because the majority of what people search for online takes place on Google. Having a great Google search ranking is very vital in SEO. Request for samples of their previous jobs to make sure they are working following the guidelines of Google.

Promising Quick Outcomes

It is not a day's job to get your website on the first page of Google. No matter what you do, this is the fact. It takes a month or more to get a favorable ranking. To get on the first page, it will require around six months or more. If any provider or firm promises you fast results, you need to find someone else.

No Knowledge of the Most Recent Trends in Digital Marketing

With regard to SEO and digital marketing, innovations always come up. Any firm or specialist you plan on using should be abreast with the most recent trends and information.

Ask questions about the recent digital marketing trends, and if the specialist is unable to answer, then you may want to find someone else.

Having One Strategy for Every Approach

SEO similar to other strategies of digital marketing is different for each organization. This is because every business has its unique needs. If a provider has only a strategy for all SEO approaches, then it won't be of assistance.

No Evidence of Previous Success

A successful SEO firm should have testimonials and case studies to show how effective their methodology is. If the provider you are trying to go with has no testimonial or case study to share, it is best you look for another provider.

Chapter 3: How to Find New Clients through Cold Calling and Other Online Methods

Cold calling is still very effective. If anyone tells you otherwise, he or she is just refusing to see the possibilities. With cold calling, you will be able to get new clients for your digital agency. It has to do with numbers, but when you can call 20 or more numbers each day, you are sure to get a few prospects who are interested in a service you provide. If you understand how to pick up your phone and dial a number, you will get your business up in no time.

What Is Cold Calling?

Cold calling has to do with the traditional means of placing spontaneous phone calls to prospective business leads with the expectation of selling a service or product to them. The call is categorized as "cold" because, before the call, the caller and recipient never have had any interaction. It is quite hard to develop the capacity to make a stranger feel comfortable and let them open up during a conversation.

Professional cold callers will have to learn to handle continuous hang-ups and rejections. It is not ideal to see cold calling as just a game of numbers. When you effectively perform cold calling, it is the means of connecting to an individual via phone in a manner that is honest, professional, and open, and offering them a reasonable proposal.

Why Do Many People Stay Away from Cold Calling?

Over the years, cold calling has become famous for the numerous hang-ups that can occur if the caller has no experience or does not handle the call the right way. The stigma associated with cold calling has further increased because of the way telemarketing invades people's personal lives.

For many, being a part of the number games of call centers as they make efforts to attain their conversion goal is an experience that is rude and disrupting. This terrible reputation of cold calling is what comes to the minds of individuals when they consider using this practice to promote the services they render. Because of the experience of being the recipient of many poorly placed cold calls, we wrongly presume that this practice is flawed and is not a great one for promoting one's business.

People to Cold Call

Before you place a call to sell the services of your agency, you need to have a few people in mind already. Consider who your top prospect may be and what your ideal client may seem like. If you were in an area filled with teachers, will it be easy for you to pitch them an online marketing service or website?

Subject to the size of your organization and the sector it is in, there are perhaps diverse methods of getting the information you require to contact these individuals. For instance, insurance agents are not required to cold call. This is because they make all their information public to get a call from someone who wants coverage.

Also, you need to make sure you are calling the person who calls the shot. You don't want to waste your agency's resources and time calling low-ranking members of the organization you want to sell your services to. This is because they don't have the power to make any decision concerning the digital marketing of the company.

If you are trying to connect to a large company with a workforce of more than 100 individuals, your target is probably the chief marketer. Your goal here won't be to reach out to junior staff members; however, you don't want to be placing calls to CEOs of organizations so huge that they are not bothered about their site. If you are contacting these large organizations, good for you. This is because they usually have a huge budget and have more knowledge of what it requires to implement marketing strategies that you can handle.

If you have to contact the gatekeeper, you need to understand how to deal with that situation also. Gatekeepers are those managing a company's incoming calls. These could be secretaries or whoever is given that role in the organization. Gatekeepers are crucial if you view things from the angle of a well-to-do business individual.

Not many individuals who are running a successful organization will want to bother themselves with every individual coming to them with sales pitches. Learning to go beyond the gatekeeper is a skill you have to become better at in addition to cold calling. Gatekeepers can give you a direct link to the decision makers, and that is why it is essential to learn to deal with them. However, you need to understand that like everything else, doing this will need lots of practice.

Common Cold Call Objections and How to Deal with Them

While cold calling, you will most likely get hung up on numerous times. This may not necessarily be a bad thing as it means your leads are not wasting your time because you know where they stand.

It's more frustrating to deal with individuals that become real prospects and lead you on for a long time without the aim of making a purchase. For many people, it can be difficult to show they are not interested in your organization, and unless you can figure out these objections, you will end up wasting your resources and time chasing these leads.

Below are some of the common objections you may deal with during a cold call and how you can deal with them:

"I don't know you."

They are cold calls because the recipient does not know you and is not expecting your call. They don't even know anything concerning your services, products, and organization. For this reason, the first words you say are vital.

Also, even if you can get past the introduction, your prospect may still be irritated, closed off, and even suspicious. He or she does not like hearing from strangers, especially those trying to sell them a service or product.

How to Overcome

The first step you need to take is to get more odds in your favor. Always keep it in mind that your prospect may have inadequate time, may not be in a good mood, or may be at work. Make it less complicated for them so that they will give you some of their time.

"I need to have a brief conversation with you concerning a product we believe suits your business. Do you mind if I ask you a few questions? I assure you it won't take up much of your time."

Then offer evidence of the excellent reputation of your agency or achievement that will astound your listener.

"We recently let out a new service for [X kind of business owners] that will help solve your [X issues] fast. We have assisted more than 1,000 organizations like yours in achieving their [X goals]."

Objections that Have to Do with Money

Other major objections you are most likely going to come across during a cold call are those relating to money. Some of these are as follows:

- "This is a bit pricey for me presently, but thank you!"
- "Our budget cannot support this purchase."
- "I don't have enough funds to invest in this."

For most prospects, the shortage of funds is the default objection. It may sometimes be a real issue they are dealing with. However, lots of times, it's just a fast way of ending a conversation as the real problem may be something entirely unrelated.

Below are a few ways you can address it:

Offer Them a Discount if They Decide to Go Further with the Process

Split the cost into fewer parts and offer them comparisons they can relate with. For example, "If you pay thirty dollars each month, you will get [X benefits] and features that will help with [X issues]."

Offer a referral or case study that boosts the proven value that your service provides. This way, you sell the value and make them think less about the cost involved.

Satisfied Client Objections

Many times, your prospect already has an agency offering the same services that you do that they are satisfied with, and the response you get is something in the lines of "Thank you, but our present agency is just fine."

This is one of the most common objections that you may come across. Your role is to convince the client that your agency offers better. You can ask questions that are not open-ended but instead offer you a yes.

For example, "If our service offers you similar benefits to the one you are utilizing currently but at a lower cost, will it interest you?"

This way, you can get the prospect to begin a conversation and talk about new options that will make their operations more straightforward.

Dealing with cold-call rejections can be difficult. This is especially the case if you don't know how to go about it. Learning to master responses and rejections are crucial for your success in cold calls.

The objections we have covered above can be of help if you consistently do the following:

- Be prepared: Put your sales scripts in order, take essential notes during calls, and record conversations you have with prospects so that you can listen later to determine areas you can improve.

- Practice: See every call like a game of numbers. Do not let failures or rejection get to you. It is a necessary step for growth.

Try your best and keep going.

- Be persistent: Give yourself a daily, weekly, or monthly target. Irrespective of how you feel, ensure you hit that target even if you make no sales. Being persistent can help you go past any obstruction down the road.

Getting Over Cold-Call Fear

Developing a fear of cold calls is normal. This is the case especially after you have received a few rejections and limited success. However, if you spend time imagining who you are going to speak to, what you are going to say, and the way the conversation is going to go, you may never pick up the phone.

Instead, there are a few steps that can help you deal with this fear. They are as follows:

Carry Out Proper Research

In the eyes of many people, cold calling does not have an excellent reputation. Most of the time, this is because cold callers do not do the necessary research. That is why this point is very vital before you dial any number.

You need to know who you are calling and what your goals are before you pick up the phone. Will the person need your services? Run a Google search for his company first. Does the name seem hard to remember? Get it in memory before you pick up the phone.

Doing some research can ensure that you and your prospect will have a comfortable time on the phone.

Be Ready for Rejection

For most cold callers, one of the main fears is picking up the phone and getting rejected after making a great pitch. You need to understand that rejection is a part of it. Not everyone you call will need the services of your agencies. Don't let it hold you back. Remember, that it is just business and nothing personal.

Make a Plan

In addition to preparing your introductory line, you need to have a plan ready for what you would cover. Try to list out your key points and have that list close before the call. Doing this will allow you to pass the information you want to without the need to overthink. This way, you can channel your focus to other areas, like being warm.

However, ensure you don't get sucked into the mistake of reading directly from a script. Even if you have placed numerous calls during the day and you are exhausted, doing this will make you sound robotic, and nobody finds that impressive.

Be Tenacious but Well Mannered

When you place a cold call, you do it with a goal, whether it is to schedule another call or to make an appointment to discuss things further. You need to move things toward your set goal fast. If you are unable to reach a person, try again as many times as possible.

The moment you can get a hold of the person, don't waste any time in politely sending the information that you want to. Respect is vital, especially when you are speaking to a gatekeeper.

Do not forget that the receiver was probably busy with other stuff before your call came in, so make sure you thank them for the time spent even if the outcome is not what you desire.

Do Not Be Discouraged by Voicemail

There is a likelihood that you will be reaching lots of your prospects' voicemails. This may not be a pleasant experience, especially when you want to get a hold of the prospect.

As annoying as this may seem, the right voicemail message covering all the appropriate areas can get you a callback. If this doesn't happen, it can at least position you for an easy follow-up call. Keep it sweet and short as this will increase the probability of your prospect listening to the entire message.

On a final note, remember that if a person says that they have no interest in what you are offering, then take them off your records totally if they ask. Not doing this can result in a huge fine if you are reported to the ICO.

Closing a Cold-Call Sale

All individuals in sales know that they have to close sales because prospects won't do it. However, you may not be aware that it is equally crucial to close your cold calls. If you want to make close calls on behalf of your agency, you need to learn how to close a cold-call sale.

The steps below can be of help even if your goal is to close for an appointment instead of a sale.

Have Specific Targets

A little knowledge can be a powerful tool. To ensure you have a great chance of getting an appointment, before you try to make an appointment or meeting with any individual, you need to have a precise idea of the following:

- Who do you want to speak to?

- What industries should they be in?

- What geographical location should they be in?

- What organization?

- What should be the target budget?

When reaching out, the responsibility and power to make specific targets are in your hands. If the person on the other end of the line has the appropriate profile, you have a better chance. But if they do not, no matter how skillful or polite you are, you have a slim chance of getting that sale.

Don't Aim to Close the Entire Sale

Trying to close the entire sale via your cold call is not the best route to go. The truth is that it hardly ever works. It is almost impossible to ultimately attain information about the needs of a prospect and provide them a solution via a single short call.

This is only possible in the slight event that you call a prospect who had plans to make a purchase but has not made a move yet. In this situation, the prospect may extend the length of the cold call to allow you to complete the entire sale in a single call. However, this is something that rarely happens.

During most of your calls, your objective should be to ensure you get an appointment with the prospect. This appointment could be a long phone call or a physical meeting. It could also be a webcam meeting. Another goal you should have during a cold call is to qualify the prospect partially during your first call so that you can minimize the possibility of wasting the prospect's time and yours if they are unable to purchase from you.

If your goal is to get the prospect to set up an appointment, your job during the entire call should be to let him or her see how beneficial a future meeting is. Prospects are not bothered about your numbers, but instead, they want to know how it benefits them. And you only have minimal time to show them via the phone. This is why during the call, you must try as much as you can to let them see the benefits you can provide.

Have an Amazing Opener

The first step when you want to close an appointment is to get the prospect to remain on the phone for as long as you need. For this reason, the most crucial part of the whole call is the first words out of your mouth.

If you can create and deliver a fantastic opener, you will pique the interest of your prospect, and he or she will want to hear you out. If you are unable to pique the prospect's interest immediately, there is a high chance that he or she will come up with a reason to drop the call when he or she finds out you are trying to sell a service.

Ask Questions

When you have kicked things off with a fantastic opener and you have the interest of your prospect, what you need to do next is to ask for his or her consent to ask some questions. You can offer this as a benefit to him or her by saying something in the lines of "I know you are a busy person, so before I obstruct your day any further, I need to be certain my service is suitable for you. Could I please ask some questions?"

Now that you have made the prospect see that you don't want to waste his or her time, he or she will have a higher possibility of hearing you out.

Finish the Close

If the prospect remains qualified after the steps above, you can begin finishing the close. Remember, it is crucial to place your scheduled appointment as something that will be of benefit to your prospect. You can openly do this by providing the prospect with a free trial of your service.

If this won't work, you need to let the prospect have a glimpse of what he or she stands to gain from using the services or products your agency offers. However, if you keep talking about the service or product, you may lose the interest of the prospect. The idea is to pique the prospect's interest just enough so that he or she will look forward to the other things you have to say during your appointment.

Other Ways to Get Clients for Your Agency

If you want to go beyond cold calling for getting clients, there are other ways to go. One of these is going online. The internet offers you vast ground to draw in clients. In this section, we will be covering the various ways you can get clients for your agency online.

Place Ads on Craigslist

Craigslist is free, and even though it sometimes get negative feedback, it still pulls in a tremendous amount of traffic. If your company is already a huge one, it may not seem like a great idea. However, if you are a start-up digital marketing agency, posting a Craigslist ad can do a lot of good in bringing you clients. Just take the time to develop a full ad that shows the benefits your service provides.

Blogging

Sometimes, to find new clients, all you have to do is make it easier for people to run into your agency or find you. Instead of advertising the service you offer, you can say something about it.

A great way of doing this is through blogging. You can build your agency and yourself into an authority in the sector by developing fantastic content. Speak about the issues in the sector or strike a conversation through blogging. You can easily do this by keeping a blog for your agency where you frequently post content and share through email newsletters and social media platforms.

You can take it up a notch by guest blogging for top websites in the industry. Note the present trends and pick smart titles if you want to make an impact. Make sure your content is credible and unique, and you will be amazed at what this can do to enhance the exposure of your agency and draw in new clients.

Rank Your Website

This is a challenging route to take mainly if you are in a huge city. However, if you are unable to rank your site, how do you plan on convincing knowledgeable prospects that you can perform this service for them? Rank your site for long-tail keywords or relevant things your customers search for.

Chapter 4: How to Scale the Business

It is not difficult to scale lots of real products with the right information. All you need to do is channel more investments in marketing, and as there is an increase in demand, you enhance your stock and alter your fulfillment logistics because of that.

But when it comes with scaling a digital marketing agency, it is a whole different concept. First, let's cover what business scaling means.

Scaling Your Business—What Does It Mean?

To elaborate on this, consider this scenario: You run a service-based organization that has just gotten a new customer. If you sign that client, your revenue goes up; however, you don't possess the required resources to serve them ultimately. Then you get the services of an additional employee to aid in managing the workload of your agency more efficiently.

Yes, your business could be undergoing growth, but it is not scaling. Even though you grew your revenue when you got a new client, your expenses also grew at the same pace. The fact is, if each sale you make needs the same effort and time as the prior sale, then you don't have a scalable business.

Your business scales when it can deal with an enhanced workload while enhancing or sustaining its efficiency. When scaling your agency, below are a few success predictors:

- elevated rates of customer retention

- having numerous streams of income

- services based on subscription

- foreseeable income

- developing a range of services and products to provide your clients

Organizations can scale when their income goes up while their cost of operation stays low. If an organization enhances its income but its cost goes up at the same pace, then it isn't scaling.

Why Is Scaling an Agency Difficult?

The truth is, some businesses are not as difficult to scale in comparison to others, but why is it more difficult to scale an agency?

First, it is not easy to sustain the appropriate balance of clients and employees. Yes, you can create safety nets using minimum contracts and periods of notice, but they are not entirely perfect. There is always the possibility of more than one client leaving your agency simultaneously. This could result in your being with too many employees and inadequate funds. The reverse is also an issue.

When you want to scale a business, it is difficult to reject new clients. However, you will soon find out that you don't have an adequate amount of manpower to properly function with those new clients if you accept too many at the same time.

Moreover, the profit margins of the average digital marketing agency are usually quite low—usually around 11%–20%, usually at the back end of these figures. The less your margin of profit, the more your vulnerability. This issue makes it difficult and risky for you to scale.

Lastly, when you are operating an agency, you have no tangible product. It won't be possible to enhance production and get more stores to sell your product. What agencies sell is time, and you will only be able to enhance the amount of time you are selling if you pay additional individuals for that time.

This does not imply that it is not possible to scale an agency, but it requires a lot of time and hard work. If you want to scale your agency, the steps below can be of help.

Plan and Evaluate

Take a comprehensive look into your business and genuinely answer this question: "Is your agency ready to grow?" You won't be able to determine what areas to change unless you determine where your agency is at the moment.

Plan the steps you need to take to enhance sales. Then imagine your orders rise instantaneously. Can your present systems and workforce successfully deal with these new orders without hassles? This is where it is vital to have a great plan.

When you want to plan, a great place to begin is with a full forecast of sales growth broken down by the income and orders you wish to generate and the number of new clients. Add a spreadsheet that further aids you in breaking down the numbers by months. If you want a realistic sales acquisition plan, you need to be more precise. Next, you do a forecast of your expenses based on infrastructure, people, technology, and systems to deal with all the incoming sales orders.

Expenses will always rise; you have to be able to foresee how and when they do. Like before, you need to add a spreadsheet of your expenses that will consist of all the expenses you require to achieve your sales forecast. Make an effort to consider all areas; you will have to do some comprehensive research to provide accurate estimates of cost. However, when you do this, your plan will be better.

Pay Attention to a Precise Market

The marketing environment is one with a lot of competition. If you want to grow your digital marketing agency, you need to be specialized. You can't solve all the needs brought to you by your clients.

If you do this, your agency will have inhibited growth because you have no specific target. If a prospect gets to the site of your agency now, what will your agency be known for?

Are You a Specialized or Full-Service Agency?

Both models are functional, but breaking even is not as easy when you are dealing with all areas of digital marketing. Becoming specialized could be the key to your success.

Ultimately, the goal of your digital agency is to focus on a precise market, then channel all its resources to serving organizations in that sector.

Use Monthly Campaigns to Develop Regular Income

Making consistent revenue is a practical approach to developing an agency that is financially buoyant. For a digital agency to be successful, it is essential for it to have a regular income. Below are some ways your digital agency can get this kind of income if you are a web agency:

- **Offering site maintenance every month:** Offering maintenance of websites alongside other services relating to digital marketing, like content marketing, Facebook ads, and Google AdWords, for your clients at a fee you negotiated beforehand means you hold on to clients and the possibility of your competition taking them from you is not as high.

- **Flexible payment plans:** As opposed to giving the client a bill for the overall amount of the services you render at once, getting the payment via installments is a better means of generating continuous revenue.

- **Web hosting services:** Hosting sites for sites alongside offering additional value on software upgrades and backup services is another method of generating continuous revenue.

Take Advantage of a Lead Magnet

Your agency requires a lead magnet, such as a template, e-book, white paper, and cheat sheet, to initiate the journey of a prospect.

Since most of the individuals using your website will not convert to leads if you don't provide them with a reason to, it is vital to develop a lead market and utilize it the right way.

You can pick any lead market of value to get the contact information of their organization. Then you can begin the development process until they want to try out the services your agency offers.

Work with Influencers

If you isolate your agencies, you may not attain success. It is essential for your agency to work alongside other influencers and agencies in your sector. How can you do this?

Host sessions on Facebook live and call on influencers to share their professional advice. They will find it surprising.

Webinars can also work well in doing this. If you run an affiliate program, you can call on influencers to aid you in promoting your offers to their followers. You can also share helpful guest posts to leading blogs in the sector to get to their audience.

Spend on Corporate Training

Companies who invest in their staff by educating and training them will have more success. Corporate training is crucial for enhancing the success of your digital agency through the following ways:

- **Keeping up with trends:** Digital marketing has to do with technologies and strategies that are continuously evolving. Many organizations urge employees to keep up with recent trends. By training your staff in groups, you will pass this same message to them, ensuring your agency speaks in unison on an issue when needed.

- **Better reputation:** Creating jobs of high quality urges an increase in client recommendations and offers a platform for your organization to be seen by prospective customers. A reputation for completing the job in a manner better than your competitors is sure to draw more clients to your digital marketing agency.

- **Enhanced productivity:** When your agency has employees

equipped with the most recent resources and information, it is sure to create jobs better than others in the same field depending on tools that are already outdated. Better jobs mean more satisfied clients, which mean increased income for your business.

Use Successful Clients to Create Case Studies

Your successful customers are excellent sources for growing your digital marketing agency. You can go further than being happy about the results you offered them.

One of the most significant resources you can take advantage of on the website of your agency is client case studies. Ensure you develop a case dedicated for showcasing all the testimonials and case studies from customers.

According to a survey carried out by eMarketer, 62.6% of the respondents were in support of the fact that case studies were great tools for the generation of leads.

Use Cross-Selling and Upselling

When you close a new client, it ensures constant growth of your agency in the long run. For this reason, it is crucial to upsell to customers who know your brand already. You don't want your customers to go after experiencing a project once. You will also be opening your organization to new streams of income if you use the right method in upselling to your client.

You don't have to seem desperate and forceful, but suggest complementary offers that will give them extra value. For example, if your client came for your Facebook ads solution, you can equally upsell a Google Ads solution to aid your client in getting the best reach on the two platforms.

The same rule is applicable when cross-selling to clients. Always provide an extra value at half the price if clients were to purchase it from other competitors or individually.

Optimize the Website of Your Agency

The website of your digital marketing agency is what defines what your agency stands for and its identity. Sadly, numerous digital marketing agencies tend to ignore the design of their website.

This is a chance for you. Begin by making the design of your website stronger, alongside the off-page and on-page SEO. In essence, ensure your website has a structure that is well laid out. Develop relevant content. Interlink significant pages on your website, and connect with other sites.

This will lead to your website having links of high quality. Do not excessively concern yourself about enhancing the business of your client that you forget about your site. Instead, the website of your agency should be ideal and appealing. It should offer value to your clients even before they decide to use your services.

Establish a Seamless Onboarding Process

It is common knowledge that clients are vital to the success of all agencies. The most crucial step in the establishment of a client-agency relationship is ensuring the process of onboarding is as seamless and direct as it can be.

From the first proposal to the start of the meeting, a remarkable process of onboarding creates a great first impression. It aids you in transforming clients who already have an interest in long-term collaborators. This proves that everything they require to go further with the contract is already available.

Send your clients satisfaction surveys to determine the aspects of the onboarding process that urged them in sealing the deal, alongside other aspects that you can still develop.

Get the Appropriate Data and Tools

When you have all you require, it can aid you in making better decisions. Technology is a vital investment as a digital marketing agency. It enhances the access you have to relevant tools and core data points. It is crucial for all agencies to search for the ideal technology and integrated system that will ensure it is less complicated for them to offer the best service.

Some of the relevant technologies that digital marketing agencies can take advance of include the following:

- tools for checking SEO ranking: MOZ, SEMrush, and Google Search Console

- tools for digital analytics: Adobe Analytics, Google Analytics, and Kissmetrics

- tools for analyzing SEO keywords: SEMrush, Google Trends, and Google AdWords

Enhance Your Prices

One of the fastest ways for your agency to earn more cash is to increase your charges. It is also crucial if you plan on investing in things that will aid you in scaling.

Most times, new agencies are often hesitant to enhance their prices because they are scared of losing clients, and this is a valid fear. This is because when you use this strategy, you are likely to use clients, but most times, it is not permanent. Long-standing higher costs should imply clients of better quality and more profit margins. In essence, scaling is less difficult.

Accurately Track Time

In addition to increasing your prices, it is essential to point out where you are losing cash. Are the employees, tasks, or clients not bringing as much profit as they are supposed to?

Employees who are not performing as expected and clients who are making excessive demands make agencies lose cash always. It is partly because of how you can quickly lose track of these losses.

It can be tedious to determine the clients that are only taking up your time or when a member of your staff is not productive enough. However, it is possible to determine this and make adjustments where needed.

Invest in Artificial Intelligence

Having a marketing strategy that is personalized in today's world is crucial to ensure your client stands out from their competitors. Artificial intelligence (AI) aims to provide you with this.

AI is linked closely to machine learning and enhancing performance via analysis of data with little or no intervention from humans. In the digital marketing sector, AI can predict what a client wants to purchase and deduce their behavior. As a result, it becomes the key to pushing conversions. It can make the buying process more straightforward. It can analyze algorithms and automate reporting to study the kind of audiences who respond to numerous ads and products.

Utilize AI technology to manage profit, track SEO performance, and offer your clients alongside their customers with experiences tailored to them. When you integrate AI into your agency, it fastens things up and enhances your team efficiency while offering precise data that is crucial for the success of your business.

Hire the Appropriate Leader

Successful digital marketing agencies, as well as those that scale effectively, all have great leaders. But the sad news is that hiring the wrong leader is very easy in all industries, including agencies.

Don't get carried away by a person who knows how to speak without the actions. During interviews, don't be worried about asking in-depth questions and don't accept responses to questions that are not straightforward.

Also, do not hire a manager that has no experience in marketing. A fantastic leader will be one who has actual hands-on experience. They should not be scared about getting their hands dirty if needed as well.

If you do not have the right individual leading the agency and directing your employees, you will battle to keep employees and clients. Also, scaling will be difficult.

Invest in Technology

Technology ensures that it is less expensive and difficult to scale a business. If you make wise investments in technology, you will gain massive economies of scale with low labor. Automation can also aid you in running your agency at a reduced cost and more effectively by reducing manual work.

You can evaluate recent products on the market that can save time and money but accommodate more volumes in each aspect of your organization. Check out accounting, manufacturing, and sales management alongside other technology systems. Ensure that you evaluate not only software but also networks and hardware, like printers, computers, and servers.

Get High-Paying Clients

Lots of individuals see the ideal clients as those whom you have worked with for a long time and who can afford to pay the cost of your services without trying to cut down your prices at every turn.

When you draw in high-paying clients, you will be able to channel more time into growing your organization, assisting your clients and getting the best of your personal life. As opposed to working all week juggling as many clients as you can, it's better to channel your energy and time to a few high-paying clients.

Additionally, when you work alongside high-paying clients, you will scale your business and will genuinely enjoy the work you do because they will make your sweats feel more appreciated.

Hire a Virtual Assistant

A great way to scale your business in a cost-efficient manner is to hire a virtual assistant. These are independent contractors who do remote work for owners of businesses. These individuals possess various skills that include creative to administrative specializations.

If your agency has an increasing amount of workload and less turnaround time, then this is the appropriate moment to scale up your business. However, as a start-up, scaling your agency may require extra resources, which include additional employees to deal with the increasing volume of work. The sad news is, for lots of new and growing companies, it can be very pricey to hire full-time staff. Instead of this, a virtual assistant can assist your agency in dealing with the increasing volume of work while ensuring the expenses that come with it remains within a reasonable budget.

Virtual assistants don't physically work with you. This means you can assign them to work anytime your agency requires. It means you don't have to concern yourself with training staff as virtual assistants already come with the training required. Additionally, virtual assistants do the job more effectively and provide excellent results.

Ensure Your Landing Page Is Optimized

Before you can provide digital marketing services with success to your clients, you need to update your landing page regularly. When you optimize your landing page, it will always bring you a high rate of conversion. Some of the core features you need for optimizing your landing page include the following:

- **Make sure you have a mobile-friendly landing page.** It is crucial for you to ensure your landing page is optimized for easy viewing on mobile as mobile users are taking over traffic on the internet. This way, clients who check out your website using their mobile devices can navigate through the landing page of your website with ease.

- **Develop a call to action.** A CTA is crucial for your landing page, especially one that is well defined. This is because it lets your audience know what actions they need to take. Your contact information should be easily accessible on your landing page too. Doing this will ensure it is less complicated for users in your site. Make sure you place the CTA beneath the landing page. When you do this, it will ensure it is easy to navigate through your site, which will, in turn, enhance the rate of conversion.

- **Simplify your landing page.** Ensure your landing page offers all the needed information to ensure users make a decision fast. You need to make sure your landing page is not filled with excess information as it will reduce its optimization. This will result in a reduced rate of conversion, which is not ideal for a digital agency.

Push for Growth

When you have set up the foundation for scaling, you need to begin to push for development. How then can you make this possible?

- Channel more investments to the marketing channels where you have the most success.

- Ask satisfied clients to endorse you to others. You can also request them to offer testimonials you can utilize on their site.

- Try to partner with agencies offering the services that you don't specialize in. You don't provide branding services? Speak to other agencies that are proficient in this area and find out if there is a way for you both to grow by assisting each other's clients.

- Also, you need to remember client retention. When it has to do with successfully scaling your business, this is more crucial that acquisition of clients.

Take a Step Back

Lastly, when you have been able to scale your agency, one of the best things you can do at that point is to take yourself out of the front lines. Try not to micromanage as you got the services of the talent in your agency for a purpose. It is either you do what you are great at, or step back and let your team take charge.

Chapter 5: Case Studies and Examples

Digital marketing agencies' case studies are fantastic ways for prospects to see your success stories. The Content Marketing Institute noted that the most recognized kind of content utilized by B2B marketers are case studies, with 47% saying that case studies were the most efficient.

Benefits of Case Studies for Digital Agencies

Having a case study offers your agency numerous benefits. Some of these include the following:

It Lets Your Present Clients See Amazing Results

Portray yourself as a professional in the services you offer. The more recognition your brand name has, the better. Doing this also aids you in making your brand unique from that of your competitors.

You Can Showcase Your Approach

For prospective clients, showcasing results you have achieved for present clients is a way of letting them understand how your process functions and the things they can expect if they work alongside you.

It Can Be a Challenge for Lots of Clients to Find a Great Agency

By showing that your agency has worked alongside brands in the sector of clients, you will be able to develop trust. For instance, a plastic creation company prefers seeing case studies from similar clients and not tech-based clients.

How Are Agency Case Studies Different from Others?

Agency case studies can aid in the generation of more leads by drawing attention to how you have assisted clients in meeting their marketing objectives. As opposed to just emphasizing the client alone, the case study of your agency should show the goal of the campaign, the strategy, and the outcomes.

Before you start to develop case studies for your agency, you have to consider the following:

Your Model Client

Irrespective of whether you state your goal or not, you need to draw in the individuals you want to work alongside. You need to tailor every aspect of your content marketing approach and case studies to your ideal clients.

If you have not created a profile for your ideal clients yet, you need to take a look at your services and the individuals who want to buy those services. If you provide numerous kinds of services with diverse clients, you can develop many case studies targeting precise clients—for instance, creating a case study for Google Ads, another for SEO, among other things.

Type of Case Study

Depending on the client you serve, you will have different case studies. Instead of assuming that one case study will symbolize all the services you offer, it is more significant to use one case study to represent every service. This is because you may not have the same ideal client.

By letting potential clients see that you can provide them outcomes in the service they require, you will be able to position yourself as an authority in that field and create credibility.

Your case study basis should be dependent on the service you offer. For every service you provide, develop an elaborate case study that relates to precise areas of every service.

The tips below can aid you in crafting an exceptional case study for all the services you provide to clients:

- Email marketing: Case studies detailing email marketing can highlight conversion rates, subscriber rate, and leads among others.

- Web design: To create a case study that details web design services, you can display your results using mobile optimization, usability, and professional design among other things.

- Content writing: To create case studies for content writing, you need to emphasize how the content you created has aided clients in achieving their objectives. The goal of the client could be to enhance web traffic, enhance leads, and enhance conversions.

- You can demonstrate outcomes by measuring page views, social shares, unique visits, and the number of leads or conversions among others.

- SEM/PPC: If the services you provide consist of SEM/PPC, then you can add statistics on income, rates of conversion, and cash saved. Utilizing precise and clear statistics helps the reader to understand better and demonstrates your outcomes without complexities.

- Social media: Case studies for agencies demonstrating social media services can show how experienced you are in numerous channels, achieving success in campaigns and social trends among others.

Reaching Out to Customers for a Case Study

There is a possibility that lots of clients would love to feature on your site, especially if in return, you offer a link to their website.

When you are through working on a campaign that has been a success and you want a client to feature in a case study, you need to request his or her permission. It is not ideal to place personal information on your website without the consent of your client.

If your client refuses your invitation, it is still possible to develop a case study while omitting their details and names. The downside to this is that some clients may think it is a fictitious case study and may find a harder time believing it as opposed to when you include the client's details.

The most appealing case studies of agencies feature the logo and name of the brand. This is because utilizing popular brand names can aid in establishing you as an authority in the sector. It also offers agencies social proof.

How to Write a Captivating Case Study

To develop a captivating story, you need more information than facts. To draw in clients, you need to do the following:

Focus on the Core Points of Your Clients

When you want to write the story of your clients, the following are a few questions you can ask:

- What were the issues they were dealing with before they started using your services? Make efforts to be specific here.

- What was the effect of these issues on their business?

- Why were their first approaches not working out?

When you have dealt with the core areas, talk about how the goal of the campaign has to do with these issues and how the services of your agency have aided them in dealing with these areas.

Offer Actionable Results and Advice

You don't have to go into complete detail when talking about your strategies. However, you can talk about how you executed your strategy and what you did as this can be of help to your audience. You need to approach this as honestly as you can.

Promote the Completed Product

When you have published the success story of your customer, the next step is to engage in a promotion. You need to promote your case studies similar to how you will promote content. Take advantage of social media for this. Make them the principal part of an email campaign. You can also repurpose them into PDF formats or blog posts. It is essential to do all you can to draw attention to them here.

Use Images

It is faster to process images as opposed to texts, so taking advantage of graphs and charts alongside data can help in ensuring your case studies are more compelling to the prospects.

Visual content can also help in breaking up texts to make it easier for the audience to understand.

Do Not Make It Complex

Make the text in your case studies easy to read. To do this, you can divide your page into segments in addition to using visual content, subheaders, and headers. All these will help in keeping your readers engaged.

Structure your content with clear segments and feature a method, objective, and result. All these will demonstrate how your services benefited your clients and will aid in keeping those who do not have explicit knowledge of what you do engaged.

Creating the Ideal Case Study

Portray your agency as an authority that provides outcomes by developing fantastic case studies that demonstrate your top examples. You need to always emphasize on outcomes that dealt with pain points, offers stats and clients quotes when conceivable, and ensure the stories are visually captivating.

By going with the steps above, you will be able to develop case studies that draw in prospective clients.

Case Studies Examples

Below are a few examples of case studies that show evidence of the possible ROI. We will be taking a look at case studies in the areas of content marketing and webinars alongside social media.

Content Marketing

ADP created a content marketing campaign that enabled them to create connections and engage with their targets via an ADP solution with the help of a diagnostic assessment tool and white papers. The campaign was able to generate more than $1 million in new sales prospects with many deals closed in the initial three months of kick-off.

Social Media

CISCO developed a listening center on social media. It listened to over 5,000 social mentions daily on Twitter, Facebook, and a host of other social platforms. Cisco could regulate external agency fees, prevent other interaction costs from partners and customers, point out new sales prospects, and enhance the productivity of teams. This listening center made over 281% ROI within five months to produce a $1,596,292 annual benefit.

Webinars

LUMEDX is a little organization in the health-care technology field with a staff of 100. It wanted to make itself unique from other competitors. They utilized webinars in creating awareness for their imaging systems product and cardiovascular information, which developed customer rapport and boosted lead generation campaigns. LUMEDX was able to enhance contact with more than 500 customers, attained a competitive edge over bigger organizations, and drove more than $600,000 in yearly sales.

Chapter 6: Set Up Your Agency's Website

The website of your agency is what helps you make a first and lasting impression on the target audience. It is the primary medium for producing leads for your business.

Some of the leading websites in the globe with the leading functionalities were created by reputable agencies. However, not many agency websites provide the same level of interaction with visitors.

Agency websites differ from the websites of other businesses. There are a few key elements that must be incorporated the right way when creating the website of agencies. This is what we will cover in this chapter among a few other things.

What You Require to Develop a Great Agency Website

To create a website for your agency, you will have to buy a domain name, pay for a hosting plan, and determine the theme you want to utilize. Next, you will develop the images, content, and portfolio items that you want to display. Below are some tips that can aid you in preparing all you will require.

Make your findings on hosting companies before you sign up for a plan. There is a range of hosting companies available. However, they do not offer similar levels of services. You can ask for recommendations from others with an agency. You can also go through hosting review sites to locate a great hosting company.

Attain your hosting plan and domain name simultaneously. Buying a domain name separate from your hosting plan is possible. However, in many situations, you will be able to attain it for free during your first year of purchasing an annual hosting plan from the company you decide to choose. It ensures that managing all your activities from one dashboard is less stressful.

Include the top jobs in your portfolio. In developing your portfolio, it may be tempting to include all projects you have worked on. However, this is not a great route to go. If you want to give potential clients the best impression, you need to select only your top pieces to display in your portfolio.

Remember to add testimonials. When getting prepared for your website, try to reach out to some of your previous clients and request that they provide you with a testimonial. It will enhance how credible you seem and make it less difficult for prospective clients to go further and entrust you with their creative projects and web design.

When you have everything in place, you need to sign up for a hosting plan and get ready to go further into developing the website for your agency.

How to Create Your Digital Marketing Agency Site

The business of marketing is a highly competitive sector. Everyone has the best sales pitch and is looking to dazzle prospective clients with their talents. This is the reason why it is vital to have a remarkable web presence. If you can grab the attention of the visitors to your website, you have a better possibility of passing the information you want across, and you can offer them the information they want and urge them to contact you.

Below are a few steps to develop a well-designed and functional WordPress website that will help you become a leader as an agency.

Develop a Strong Call to Action (CTA)

A CTA can be your best friend, especially as an agency. You can include a Contact Us button below. It is a great addition as it can encourage visitors to take action. Some themes like the TopSEO theme even allows you include a link for a "Free SEO Scan" in the header. This is an excellent addition as it can take you around the whole website. Using a range of methods to inspire viewers to take action can be of considerable significance to lead generation.

Develop Interactive Aspects

When developing a website for your digital agency, it is ideal to use great typography, great layout, and appealing images. However, you can take this a step further by including some interactive aspects like what the Sonno theme offers. This theme comes alongside with an interface that gives you the chance to click on an item and enlarge it to view additional details. Adding a few extra touches similar to these go a long way in enhancing the whole user experience.

This theme comes with other amazing features, like a functional contact form, the YouTube API, and a selection of layouts for your homepage among others.

Include Service Lists That Are Easy to Follow

A great feature to include on your website is a list of services you offer. When doing this, it's best to go with a list that is concise, simple, and visually attractive. To take it further, you can easily link it to another page with more detailed information. However, the goal here is to offer users a list that they can easily read so that they do not get overwhelmed.

Let the Website Be Personal

If your prospective client is going to trust you with their needs, then it is essential they should know about who they are working with. Including personal touches like a picture and information of the CEO of the company together with other personal details can aid in developing in a real bond. Many clients will instead work with agencies they trust and know as opposed to mysterious ones. This can help in personalizing the experience for them.

Include Case Studies

Case studies can help you show your prospects your capabilities as opposed to telling them. Including details about your previous successful projects can go a long way for your agency. A theme like SEO Rocket comes with a filterable project portfolio that you can use when including case studies on your website. It also comes with a range of custom widgets, layout options, and shortcodes among others.

Include an Informative Blog

Learn to keep present and prospective clients up to date about the recent trends in the industry. This can aid in transforming you into a reliable information source. The Startuper theme comes alongside a blog layout that can offer you a way to communicate with your audience. You can also share your post on social media channels to aid you in developing your following.

This is ideal for websites that are not too large. This is because it only allows for a single level of navigation. It also comes alongside a visual composer that you can set up as a multipage or single-page website.

Elaborate the Process

A crucial part of sales is to ensure your clients are comfortable with what you are providing. This is why explaining the steps involved in your process is vital. Clients will have more confidence in your skills if they are aware of what is going to occur and when.

State Your Prices Clearly

Pricing tables are essential for contemporary web design. If you provide more than one service package, it is ideal to be straightforward and offer prospects with a list that is appealing and not difficult to read. This has to do with developing trust. The Lead Injection theme can offer you just this. It features a visual composer and about six layouts among other great features.

Develop Distinct Visuals

The objective of every website should be to have fantastic content and present it appealingly. Enhanced presentation combined with great typography can ensure you have a fantastic website.

A theme like Caliber can aid in your presentation. It comes with custom footers and headers, a page builder, and the capacity to develop custom sidebars.

Share Genuine Testimonials

Testimonials of many individuals may not seem functional; however, there is a reason numerous websites still take advantage of them. The reason is simple; they are functional. The Kudos theme offered by WordPress can help with this. It comes with a testimonial slider where you can incorporate your client testimonials. However, it is crucial that you use genuine testimonials from real clients. It counts to be genuine.

Kudos comes with over 20 homepage layouts, parallax scrolling, and WooCommerce support among other things.

Creating a fantastic website takes a lot of effort that will allow you to place the ideal agency for your prospective clients. However, you need to include a range of pieces to create a seamless website. You need to consider the content, functionality, and look of a website to create the ideal picture you desire. The steps above can ensure you get a head start into developing a fantastic website.

Chapter 7: Brand Strategy

Branding the Agency

A brand is an idea, service, or product that is publicly unique from other services, ideas, and products to ensure you can communicate and market it with ease. A brand name connotes the unique concept, product, or service. Branding has to do with the circulating and creation of the brand name. It is possible to apply branding to the overall corporate identity, as well as service names and individual products.

There are numerous benefits you stand to gain from sustaining a strong brand for your agency. Below are some of the major ones you can expect when your agency has a great brand.

Customer Recognition

When you have a strong brand, it can help you develop customer recognition. This implies that when a client is in search of a specific company to provide a service or sell a product, they recognize that your agency offers this service. Customers have more tendency to go with a brand they know as opposed to one they have never come across. This is the case even if they don't have much information about your agency or organization at that moment.

It Offers You a Competitive Edge

Your brand tells you apart from others in the marketplace. When clients support and recognize your brand, it aids in providing your agency with a competitive advantage. The more the recognition you get, the easier it is to develop your brand, and the more you will observe that your brand can compete with other popular brands.

Seamless Introduction of New Services and Products

Loyal clients and a strong brand will ensure that the products and services will cost less. It is challenging to bring in new services or products; thus, you need to test them before you channel more resources into them. If your agency has a devoted brand following, your clients will usually be interested in your upcoming services and will even look forward to your releasing them.

It Enhances the Loyalty of Customers

A strong brand helps you develop more loyalty among customers. Lots of customers are drawn to brands they have similar values with. When you develop a great brand, you have to send these values across to develop a connection with clients emotionally. Brand loyalty can last for a long time and even be transferred to the subsequent generation.

More Credibility

When you have a renowned and reliable brand, it increases your credibility with your industry, clients, and the overall marketplace. As you develop your credibility, you also develop loyalty, brand recognition, and competitive advantage. They all go together, and you will find out that your level of credibility is directly connected to your client's ease of purchase. People want to make purchases from organizations they know, like, and trust. If you have a credible brand, you have more tendency of getting the sale.

What Is a Brand Strategy?

A brand strategy is an action plan that businesses utilize in differentiating their services, identities, and products from those of the competitors. A brand strategy helps you in pointing out the picture you want to develop for your clients. This means considering the kinds of expectations and feelings you want clients to link with your agency or business.

Is your plan to be funny or professional? What if you want to be classy?

A brand consists of all the feelings and thoughts that develop in the mind of your clients when they think about your company. A brand strategy is your way of changing the way they see you till they go with the goals of your company.

Elements of a Brand Strategy

As stated by experts, a great brand can result in an enhanced company image, an increase in customer identity, and an identity that is easier for clients to relate with.

As more clients keep differentiating between businesses using the experiences they have and the way they feel as opposed to product features and price points, a brand could be the initial step of getting a competitive advantage. However, what you need to figure out is how to develop a brand that sends a message to your followers.

Before you begin channeling investments to branding consultancy and social media branding, you need to note that to create a successful brand, it needs to consist of the features below:

Purpose of Your Company

The leading agencies have something that drives them that goes beyond those everyday things that differentiate them from other agencies. If you can clearly define the purpose of your agency, you can start to develop a brand strategy that is in line with the core vision and goals of your agency. While obvious purposes like earning money are crucial to any organization or agency, clients have a more powerful connection with brands that want to go further than just attaining a considerable paycheck.

Consistency

When you have determined what keeps your brand going, you need to keep going with those ideas and offer your clients a consistent identity. As stated by studies, when a brand presents itself consistently, it has four times higher likelihood to benefit from brand visibility.

You may believe it is difficult to achieve consistency. However, this is not the case. It just means you need to evaluate everything you do and ask yourself if it goes with the image you are portraying to those around you. For example, if you have chosen to give yourself a refined and professional identity, then posting funny videos and memes on your Facebook wall may not be the way to go.

A fantastic method of enhancing your possibility of consistency is to develop a few guidelines for your brand. You need to note that consistency in the image of your brand is crucial for your internal communications plan because it aids in strengthening your fundamental vision and messages with your staff.

Emotional Connections

Customers include more emotions than you may believe when making purchases. Also, B2B brands make more sales when they take advantage of emotional marketing messages as opposed to logical ones. Emotion is a crucial element that enhances how great branding strategies are. If you can locate a means of creating connections with your clients at a much deeper level, you will be able to improve engagement and develop a relationship that is easier to maintain for the long run.

An organization that utilizes emotions to create strong relationships with client is Apple. It uses a branding strategy that takes advantage of simplicity and a need for development to create connections with a broad audience. Apple is influential because it calls on the need for humans to be included in something that is beyond them. Apple understands the need for humans to be social and their desire to be included in a crucial group dynamic. This is the reason why individuals stay on lines for days to get the most recent Apple releases.

Empowerment of Employees

Although your clients are a crucial element when it has to do with ensuring your agency is successful, there is also a group of individuals often ignored in the business world, and those are your employees.

Customer insights are crucial if you want to attain success. This is the case irrespective of whether you are developing a brand from the start or investing in a new kind of social media branding. Incorporating a brand advocacy strategy can aid you in creating a more powerful brand image. The truth is that numerous individuals having the same thing to say about an organization are easier to believe compared to a single voice. Additionally, your marketing messages will reach more people when they are shared by the staff.

Employee advocacy can help reinforce the values and culture of your company that you talk about in your About Us page and press releases, showing how you transform them into actual campaigns and behaviors.

How to Develop a Brand for Your Agency

Irrespective of the field you are in, having a strong brand is crucial. If your agency has a strong brand, it will offer your business focus. It will also help you in describing your firm, the services you provide, and others.

If you understand what you are and who you are, it will be easier for you to determine the prospects to chase and those to ignore. These and many more are reasons why creating a strong brand is essential. The steps below will aid you in developing a strong brand for your agency.

Audit Your Brand

Irrespective of how large or small your agency is, your website visitors, clients, and followers on social media already have a way they see your brand.

Most times, there is a disparity between the way you want to see yourself and the way the clients see you. Branding typically has to do with the perception you have of yourself to that of your customers.

Before you move any further into branding, you need to do a comprehensive brand audit. Evaluate all areas of your brand, its present perception, and the entire brand cohesiveness. When you do this, it will aid you in understanding your present standing and the areas you need to change for the future. The following can help with a brand audit:

Ask Your Clients Questions

Understanding the way your website visitors, clients, and followers on social media see you is a crucial aspect of any brand audit. You can do this via numerous methods, including the following:

- Develop an online poll and provide it to all email subscribers, website visitors, and followers on social media.

- Interview customers so that you can understand the way they see your brand and yourself.

- Pay attention to conversations on social media and monitor keywords to see the way people define you.

As regards insights, you will get the most information from interviews. However, they are also the most difficult to prepare. It is less difficult to run online polls, but the data they provide is limited.

A fast method of getting insight is to utilize a tool for social media monitoring to view how others are speaking of your brand. Search for keywords that showcase the negative or positive experiences of your brand. If you have a massive number of followers, you can take advantage of a tool for social listening to see the keywords that have to do with your brand that people are using.

If you decide to go through the direction of a poll/interview, the following are a few questions you can ask:

- Is our brand experience or website unique from that of others?

- Why did you choose to collaborate with us? How did our brand help with this decision?

Finally, ensure you monitor all replies in another spreadsheet.

Appraise Your Competitors

Customers will make an opinion of your brand using your competitors as a bar. For this reason, it is reasonable to add the evaluation of your brand in your brand audit.

You can begin by putting down your major competitors. Group them using the following categories:

- specialization: if they are focused on a niche or a full-service agency

- location: if they serve global or local clients

- target market: the type of customers they serve

With this information, you will be able to pinpoint your aspiring and direct competitors. Note that direct competitors are those agencies that have the same niche, size, and target market as you, while aspiring competitors are developed agencies you hope to be like.

Take a look at the way those competitors branded their agency. Check out their websites, marketing collateral, and presence on social media. You can also read their blogs, sign up for their newsletters, and follow their pages on social media.

Ask yourself the following:

- Is their brand messaging, design, and copy cohesive and consistent?

- Do they use professional, quirky, or funny copies?

- Does their brand image go with their price point and target market?

Evaluate Your Present Brand

Next, you need to ascertain what you believe of your brand. Do you convey this perception via your marketing collateral? To answer this, you need to begin by collecting all aspects of your brand. It should consist of the following:

- website copy and design

- logos

- email newsletter and blogs

- marketing collateral, like white papers, e-books, and case studies

- sales collateral, like rate sheets and brochures

- social media messaging

- style guides, email signatures, and communication plans

Typically, any aspect of your agency that gets to a customer should be included in your analysis. After collecting all these, you need to evaluate them using the following:

- expectations—for instance, if the identity of your brand goes with the expectations of your clients

- consistency—if all the elements of your brand are cohesive and uniform

- clarity—if your positioning is passed through the elements of your brand

Any component that does not pass the value of your brand will break the experience. Note all these elements before you head to the subsequent step.

Point Out Where You Want to Be, Where You Are, and Where You Are Meant to Be

Before developing your brand, you have to determine the type of digital marketing agency you want to operate. You will need to have an in-depth look at yourself to find your vision and values. You can also ask your entire staff and ask stakeholders, including clients and investors, for ideas.

The crucial thing to do is to fit the agency you can develop into that you want to develop. A fantastic agency is created when your interest fits with your market trends and expertise. It is essential to include recent market trends in your brand identity. Taking advantage of the rising trends, like drones and social mobile, can aid you in developing a distinct brand and make you unique from competitors.

Also, create a list of the expertise you are presently able to access, both freelance and in-house. If you plan on becoming specialized, you need to make sure that you have the skills.

When you are through with this, clearly put down your philosophy, mission, and values.

After covering this, you can now go on to developing the brand for your agency.

Here are the steps you need to take:

Determine Your Brand

If you have carried out an audit of your brand by now, you will have an idea in mind of what you want your brand to be. Here, you will take this a bit further. Begin by carrying out an analysis of the following:

- What is the type of clients you have drawn in till now?

- What is the type of customers you want to draw in?

- What are your employees proficient in? What do they love doing best?

- Are there any market gaps you could provide service to? Any rising technology you could become proficient at?

- What do your employees or yourself detest doing the most? This is a question lots of agencies overlook. But it is very vital as it is impossible to develop an organization based on something you have no love for.

With this information, begin a sketch of your brand. A great way of doing this is to develop a brief and compelling mission statement.

Together, the vision and mission statements are the how, why, and what of your organization.

Strike a Balance between Implicit and Explicit Branding

Your brand is a merge of the things you say and things you don't. The things you say include your vision and About Us page. You are clearly or explicitly informing people of what your brand entails. It should consist of things potential clients can quickly read through to attain an idea of what your brand is all about. These could include keywords like *vibrant, bold*, and *amazing* among others.

Past this, your brand also consists of implicit elements, which include your client list, design, and chosen images among others. They are the things you don't say.

Your aim should be to ensure both your explicit brand statements and implicit elements align with each other. If you say you are professional and your website is filled with cartoons, then you are not doing justice to your brand. When you begin developing the identity of your brand, ensure you have this balance in mind.

Get Ideas from Your Competitors

Although you need to make efforts to be unique, don't forget to find out what your competitors are doing. They may just have found the perfect means of drawing in target clients.

It is not always a terrible idea to get inspiration from your competitors. This is especially the case in industries with a high level of competition where there is a high demand for the attention of a potential client.

There is a possibility that your competitors who have been successful have probably tried out the leading approaches to get to their target audience. If all the information and data shows that a particular approach is what is in vogue, you may not make any headway if you try something else.

When studying your competitors, observe the following:

- what type of clients they draw in

- how they portray themselves to these customers

Search for alignment of client image. If a competitor states that they have worked alongside HP to develop a youthful, bold, and fresh redesign, can you find anything in the image of their brand that portrays these values? If yes, what copy, colors, and UX did they utilize in showcasing these values?

Use this information as ideas for your brand, especially if you plan to draw in the type of customers other competing agencies have.

Be Sure of Consistency

If you take a look at some of the most influential brands in the world, you will see a similarity; when it comes to their brand messaging, they are incredibly consistent.

You will instantly recognize these brands because of how consistent their brand presence has been till date.

When it comes to agency consistency, it means the following:

- consistency in the way they communicate
- consistency in copy
- consistency in design

Every aspect of your brand that your customer comes in contact with should possess a cohesive and consistent message. If the colors of your brand are purple and yellow, your logo, blog, Facebook cover image, and email signatures should include these colors. If you label yourself as professional, your tweets and website copy among others should resonate these.

Importantly, you need to be consistent with the way you communicate with every stakeholder. Develop a plan for communication with a style guide clear enough for each member of your team to follow. All the messages being sent to clients should go with this guide.

To get ideas, you can go through the identity guidelines of well-known brands. To begin, check out the identity guideline of Samsung.

Showcase Your Projects, People, and Passions

When you are running a business when your products are individuals, it becomes a major aspect of your brand to showcase them. There are two parts to this:

- showcasing your work
- showcasing the expertise, knowledge, and culture that make it possible to do your work

When it comes to creative agencies, it becomes even more crucial to do the second because creative thinking is often as a result of the culture that encourages it.

So what are the available options of showcasing your culture to enable you to incorporate it in your brand image?

One way of doing this is to take advantage of social media. Make your presence on social media, especially all those channels with a massive level of visual, like Facebook and Instagram, an aspect of your brand identity. Utilize these platforms in showcasing the culture of your company, side projects, client projects, and other things that portray your beliefs, ambitions, and interests.

You are offering clients a peek of what interests your people, what they are like, and what their passion projects, as well as yours, are. Social media is an incredible means of getting this done.

Social media helps you go beyond telling; it lets you show as well. Developing a good brand involves a lot more work. However, an elaborate brand audit along with these tips will give you a head start in the creation of your brand.

From here, you can adjust, grow, and develop a brand that captures your vision. If you want to learn more about creating a great brand for your business, check out the book _Instagram Influencer Marketing Secrets_, which covers this topic in detail.

Chapter 8: How to List Your Business on Google My Business

Including your business to Google is a process that is free and quick. It helps you get your organization out there. It is a free means of advertising locally that is waiting for you to exploit. Google My Business is a seamless way of ensuring your clients can find you when they run a search on Google or Google Maps. In this chapter, we will be covering how you can develop your Google business listing.

Why Should You Promote Your Business on Google?

With regard to search results, you would want your business to feature on the first page of Google. Over 3 billion individuals are taking advantage of Google to get their daily needs. That is more than 70% of every search online. More than half of these searches take place via mobile devices. Individuals are always searching for what they require in places close to them at the present moment.

This moment is a great one for businesses running locally. Clients are using Google to locate your product or service locally in massive amounts, and Google is providing you with the opportunity to advertise your business for free on their platform, which is the largest one out there.

How then do you take advantage of this great opening? The steps below can help you with that. But first, let us take a look at what Google My Business is about.

What Is Google My Business?

This is a tool for local listing that helps you develop the online presence of your business for free. It allows you to feature on Google Maps, Google Search, as well as the useful Local Pack.

This tool offers you the chance to tell your story, develop brand awareness, display your business, and promote exclusive sales and occasions using video, photos, and other things.

When you claim and verify your Google My Business listing, your clients can locate you, and you can offer what they are searching for.

What you need to do first is to search for your business name on Google to find out whether it has already been claimed by someone else or whether it is still available. If a Google My Business listing shows up, it means someone else has claimed your business.

If the latter is the situation, you have no issues. Google can aid you in reclaiming your listing. We will be covering all these in detail later in this chapter.

Create Your Listing on Google

There are two core rules to note to ensure that Google promotes and identifies your business. These are the following:

- You need to be consistent: your name, phone number, and address have to be the same one on your website and other social media platforms.

- You need to be accurate: your name, phone number and address, events, opening hours, location, and your complete business information have to be accurate.

If no one has claimed your business listing, the next step is to create your Google listing for free. The initial steps are the most important ones, and you need to ensure your business information is accurate as we have covered earlier.

When you start the creation of your listing, you will be required to fill out the details of your business, which include the following:

- The name of your business: This is straightforward. Put down the legal name of your business into the field provided.

- Your location: You need to put in a physical local business address where individuals can find you if they have to. It's not ideal to use a virtual address or PO Box here.

How to Include Your Business to Google Maps

When you have included your location, Google will instantly show you the area and give you a pin for your area. All you need to do is drag this to your exact business location and click on next. When you add your business and location to Google My Business, you are now on the most utilized service for navigation on the Web.

Select Your Category

Google has more than 10,000 categories you can pick from that are constructed to aid your customers in finding your exact offering and locate your business. Make efforts to choose as little categories as you can. Do not forget to be very specific.

If you are a Mexican restaurant, don't just fill in "restaurant." Let your clients find precisely what they are searching for. Also, don't let your choice be redundant. For instance, don't select both "restaurant" and "Mexican restaurant." Google does not find this appealing.

If you notice that you are unable to go any further and need some help, Google My Business support provides terrific advice on optimizing and picking your category.

Include the Contact Information You Want Everyone to See

It is preferable to use a phone number in addition to a local area code on Google if you can. Google does not support toll-free numbers, but it's always best to follow the principles of Google.

When including the URL of your website, make sure you are the owner of the website and not a third-party website. It also should not be your profile page on social media. Google prefers that you link your website directly. Also, ensure that the details you fill in your Google My Business listing are no different from what is on your website.

Now that you have included the necessary information about your business, you can now head to the next step of verifying your business.

How to Claim Your Business on Google

When including the name of your business into the dashboard of Google My Business, it is likely to show up in the drop-down menu. If you notice this, it implies that someone else has already listed this business even though you have not developed the presence.

It will still be necessary for you to claim and verify your listing. This is to enable you to take charge and alter your account on Google business.

Unclaimed Listing

Do a quick search on Google for your business. If you have not developed a listing and one shows up, it may be surprising, but it does not need to be. Any individual using Google can develop a Google My Business profile, and this could have been the situation. If you see the "Own the business?" link on your listing, it means it hasn't been claimed, and all you need to do is click it.

When you click this, you will be led through some steps that are similar to creating your listing on Google My Business. All you need to do is go with the above steps and take charge.

Listing Already Claimed

If someone else has claimed the listing, you will see a message with an incomplete email address. If you have the details, all you need to do is log in to Google My Business with that email address and make changes to your listing.

If this email address does not seem like the one you remember, click Request Access and go with the provided options. When you have filled in your details in Google, a confirmation mail will be sent to you. The individual who owns that listing will also get a Google mail to contact you and clear up everything. You will also be provided with a link from Google in your confirmation email that will give you the capacity to monitor your request status.

If you are facing problems, like not getting feedback from the owner of the registered listing, Google support offers you additional information.

Verify Your Business

Now that you are through creating and claiming your Google listing, the next step is to verify your presence.

Google will offer you a pin for verifying your account, which you can then fill in to finish the last step. To ensure owners of any business can take advantage of this opportunity, Google will give you the chance to select from a range of methods to attain this pin.

- Mail: You can request for a postcard to be delivered to your address. It takes 5–14 days for delivery, and you must verify the listing in 30 days.

- Text or call: If you go with this method, you will get the pin, and all you need to do is follow the instructions that follow.

- Video verification: To help you verify your account, Google can set you up on a video call with an expert.

- Email: There are businesses wherein Google will send pins directly to their inboxes. You can also click on the verification link that you get.

- Instant verification: This is a faster route to take. However, you need to be registered with some other Google service to be qualified for this method.

Once you have covered this step, you have been able to verify your account successfully. You can then take advantage of all other platforms offered by Google.

How to Optimize Google My Business Listing to Ensure Success

Now that you set up your listing, the next step is to optimize it so that you can begin getting higher rankings. The steps below can help you with this:

Take Advantage of the "Google Posts" Feature

Google posts are similar to mini ads or posts on social media for your business that come up on Google Maps and the local panel. To create these, you can do it via your Google My Business dashboard. The great news is that they instantly come up in your local search results. All posts can be as much as 300 words, and the best part is that you can include a GIF, image, and a CTA button.

To use this feature to its full capacity, you can utilize Google posts for the following:

- If you are running an event, create a post with all the information and include a link to your registration page.

- Are you launching a new product, or do you have a specific sale? Create a post with high-quality images including all the details.

- Recently published a blog post? Widen your reach and add a link and brief description in a post.

The possibilities are limitless and come with a host of CTA buttons that include the following: Reserve, Sign Up, Get an Offer, Learn More, and Buy. When you are through verifying your Google My Business account, your posts option will show up in the menu of your dashboard, waiting for you to exploit it.

When developing your post, you need to consider the following:

- You have a word count limit of 300, and the initial 60–70 words will be displayed on desktop and mobile if you utilize a CTA button. Ensure you use them properly.

- If you don't add a CTA button, the entire 300 words will show up on your mobile.

- This is developed for your clients to ensure the information you include is readable. Don't use terms that are too technical. Use language that they can easily understand.

- When you have developed your post and clicked publish, you can take a look at your recent posts waiting to be viewed by individuals in search of your business.

Create Connections with Your Clients via Messaging

Google lets you potential clients and clients send you direct messages and vice versa. Although you provide your phone number on Google My Business, they may not call your business every time.

According to studies, more individuals engage using texts, with over 90% of texts being read in five seconds after it is sent. This can be a fantastic opening for you to enhance personalized customer engagement and have an extra edge over your competitors.

Not every business owner would like individuals to text their lines. With the Google Allo App, you will be able to use the same number linked to your Google My Business account. This is an excellent method of separating your personal and business text messages.

This feature lets you have a one-on-one connection with your clients, provide them responses to queries, enhance customer loyalty, and respond to comments. By letting your business be seen as more transparent, you will be able to enhance your credibility and eventually sales.

Be Informed about Your Insights

Google provides you with insights into the way customers see your business. If you want to understand how your online efforts are going, these analytics are crucial. They also help you in understanding how to optimize how clients are engaging with your presence online.

Google aids in breaking down the way your clients find you irrespective of whether they search directly for the address or name of your business (direct search) or they search for a service or product you provide and locate your listing (discovery search).

Google will also inform you which clients directly check out your website, view your pictures, ask for directions to your location, and call you. Google will also inform you precisely where clients are requesting directions. This will point you to the geographical location of your clients. Being informed about your insights will provide peak impact and provide your Google My Business listings with a great digital strategy.

Add Videos and Photos

Your profile picture is the first thing clients will come across. The role of your picture is to urge users to want to learn more about your organization. Irrespective of whether it's your storefront or logo, make sure that the image is of high quality and demonstrates the quality your agency stands for and provides. Studies state that listings that have high-quality images have twice the likelihood to be categorized as reputable and have over 30% more clicks.

Photos feature has been in existence for some time, and using user-generated images is an amazing way to make your brand less robotic and develop a community. User-generated images of excellent quality help in creating interaction with your agency and can offer you lots of content to use in your photo gallery.

Video, on the other hand, is a very new feature. Now, you will be able to add a 30-second video to highlight your agency directly to Google. Google has created guidelines to make sure your videos relate directly to the location of your business. This is a great chance to share your organization to prospective clients in a personalized way.

Use Reviews

Google urges reviews, and these reviews can help inspire prospective clients. Eighty percent of customers find reviews as reliable as personal recommendations while 90% of clients go through local reviews, and over 60% of clients leave reviews for local businesses.

Google My Business drives the process of reviews and makes it less complex by offering a link from the dashboard of your Google My Business, which you can then send to clients, requesting they leave a review.

Leaving a response to every review is crucial. It lets prospective clients know you care and value your present clients. If you get a bad review, it can be a good thing as it presents you with an opening. When you respond to a negative review, it can aid you in noting possible problems with your business and still urge your prospective clients to go with your agency or business. Studies state that 44.6% of clients will still go with a business that has a negative review they leave good response to. It does not matter if the reviews are negative or positive. When you respond to every one of them, it shows an exceptional level of customer service.

A very vital gateway for clients to locate your local business offline and online is Google search. By taking advantage of Google My Business, it puts all the information concerning your business in the eyes of prospective clients already in search of your products and services. It is impactful, powerful, and free for you to use and set up. It may be to the detriment of your business if you do not exploit this great opportunity.

By not claiming your Google My Business listing, you are providing other competitors the chance to have a lead on your agency.

Chapter 9: Using Facebook Ads

What Is Facebook Ads?

A Facebook ad is a tool that gives businesses the capacity to market to over one billion users on Facebook each month. Ads can be as complicated or as simple as they desire. It is a straightforward process to use Facebook ads as it lets users target their audience via self-serve tools. Moreover, it offers them an analytics report that monitors the performance of every ad.

The visibility and reach can aid in leveling the playing field of your agency and that of your clients who want to compete with other similar organizations that do not have a budget. With the Business Manager platform that Facebook offers, businesses have a one-stop platform for all their advertising and marketing requirements. Additional features like access to product catalogs and Instagram are included in the mix.

To master advertising on Facebook, it needs a comprehensive understanding of how to use the platform in all areas. We will be covering all this in the information contained in this chapter.

Types of Facebook Ads

Agencies can take advantage of numerous kinds of ads Facebook offers. Below are a few of them:

Sponsored Story

A sponsored story is developed when a client interacts with a brand. It functions just the way an organic story does, only that the Facebook friends of the users will be able to view the ad. You can alter the target audience using gender, audience, and location. This can help your agency in reaching the appropriate audience.

Sponsored Ads

Unlike a sponsored story, these are the voice of the organization. You are responsible for the creation of ads and control the audience and content. You can develop page post ads or standard ads, depending on which they choose.

Sponsored Posts

These are regular posts that owners of businesses pay to be transformed into an ad. This kind of post could be simple. For instance, a post speaking about the history of the business.

Carousel Ads

With these kinds of ads, advertisers can display three to five videos, pictures, or both in one post. Advertisers will be able to feature one lengthy image or numerous products.

Canvas Ads

These are mobile-optimized, full-screen ads that feature a mix of links, images, texts, and videos for the best user experience. These kinds of ads are very interactive. Users can pause, pan in and out, swipe, and click without heading outside Facebook.

How Can Facebook Ads Benefit Your Agency and Your Clients?

The following are some of the benefits Facebook ads can provide.

Modified Targeting

Facebook provides you with a range of targeting options to ensure you only display your ads to a specific audience. This could be based on location, demography, similar audiences, behaviors, and other things.

With the Facebook ad manager, it is less difficult to deal with advertising campaigns on social media channels. With straightforward clicks, running ads across Instagram, Facebook, and many others will be a breeze. You will also be able to incorporate a tracking pixel into pages in your website to enable you to target your perfect clients with the products they have the most interest in.

Huge Mobile Audience

The popularity of smartphone is continuously on the rise, which makes mobile traffic crucial. Lots of people are always on their mobile devices during periods of the day, which ensures you have a vast mobile audience to tap from.

Comprehensive Analytics

Facebook offers you detailed reporting and analytics for the performance of ads. As opposed to battling to see your rate of conversion, it helps you state it out clearly. With the Insights tab, you will be able to view posts with the top performance and page likes among others. You can equally measure your page with that of your competitors to see how you are meeting up.

The data visibility gives you the chance to alter a campaign as you desire as opposed to learning it was not effective after all the efforts.

Enhanced Brand Awareness

Lots of Facebook users go through their newsfeeds numerous times daily, which gives your desired audience recurrent contact with your ads.

Even if at first they do not click through, the recurrent ad visibility aids in developing trust. It also establishes retargeting chances for you later on.

Running Facebook Ads on Behalf of a Client

At some point in your agency, you will have to run an ad for a client. This is one of the ways you make revenue. So how do you get this process started?

Below, we will be taking a look at two vital steps required before you begin to run ads for other people. You can equally explain these steps to your clients, so they understand what they are required to do before you begin.

Become the Administrator of Their Facebook Page

There are a few ways a person can become an admin of your Facebook page. Note that you can do these steps with the right permission of the client.

To do this, head to the Facebook page and pick the Page Roles from the column by the left. Next, include the email address used by the person to log in to Facebook from the Admin Roles screen and save it. It is ideal to place the admin role as "Editor" if they want to post something they will advertise later on or develop an event they want to advertise. If you are certain that later on, your client won't develop any content, then you can pick the "Advertiser" role.

Now, it is required that you have to be connected as friends on Facebook if you want to include them as your page admins. If you are working with the Facebook Business Manager, it will be required that you add the individual in your Business Manager and offer them admission to your Ads account and Page. Once you have given them access, the status will display "Pending." If you included a person and they did not receive a notification, they need to check out the Invites area on Facebook to see if there is an invitation pending.

Become an Admin of the Client's Facebook Ads Account

Next, you need to ensure you run the ads via the Facebook Ads account of your client as opposed to yours. You can get this done by becoming an admin on their account. This is not the same thing as being their page admin.

For you to get the role as an admin on the ad account of the client, it is essential for the client to select the wheel in the top right corner and pick Manage Ads.

From the top left corner, pick the settings after expanding the menu. You may need to pick All Tools to view all of it. Next, move to Ad account roles and click Add People. A pop-up box will come up, and it will prompt you to include the individual's email. Note that it has to be the same mail they used in logging into Facebook. If you are connected as friends on Facebook, you can begin by typing in their name. It may not be as straightforward if you are not connected as friends. Ensure you select the Ad Account Advertiser so that you will be able to run ads.

After your business with your client is done, get the client to take you off as an admin from their ads and page account. This safeguards you and your client from any problems that may come up along the line. You also have the option of removing yourself as an admin.

How to Advertise for Your Clients on Facebook

After covering the steps above, now it's time to develop a Facebook ad campaign on behalf of your clients. The following are the steps to take:

Pick the Client's Objective

Head to the Facebook Ads Manager. Log in and pick the Campaigns tab, then select Create to begin a new Facebook ad campaign.

Facebook provides 11 marketing objectives, depending on what your client wants to achieve with the ad. They include the following:

- brand awareness

- traffic

- app installs

- video views

- catalog sales

- conversions

- lead generation

- engagement

- reach

- messages

- store visits

Select a campaign objective, depending on the goal of your client for this specific ad. Note that for objectives like sales for conversion, you will have to pay per action. However, objectives like views and traffics will require you to make payment for impressions.

Give the Campaign a Name

Scroll downward to give the Facebook campaign a name. Next, you have the option of choosing whether to develop an A/B split test. Also, you will have the option of choosing whether to put on budget optimization. This can be a significant option if you are utilizing various ad sets.

To head to the next step, select Set Up Ad Account.

Set Up Your Ad Account

If you have set up an account already, this step will not come up, but if this is the first Facebook advert, you will have to include some vital account details. Put in the country of your client, the time zone, the currency of choice, and select Continue.

You need to be careful when making a choice here. This is because if you want to alter your choices, later on, you will need to create another ad account.

Target Your Audience

Above this screen, you will be required to give your Facebook ad campaign a name and decide the page you want to get promoted. Scroll downward to begin developing your ads target audience. The first option you will see is to include a custom audience of individuals who have already had some interaction with your business on Facebook and off Facebook.

Begin by picking your target age, location, language, and gender. As you select your options, observe the audience size indicator on the right-hand side of the screen, which offers you an idea of your potential ad reach.

Next, you need to move to comprehensive targeting. You need to have it in mind that effective targeting is crucial for maximizing return on investment, and with the help of Facebook paid ads, you are privy to a lot of targeting options.

You are privy to two options to help your client ensure their audience is as precise as they desire. They include the following:

- Detailed targeting: With this field, you can exclude or include people using interests, demographics, and behaviors. At this point, you have to be precise. For example, you can decide to target individuals who have an interest in both running and jogging but exclude those that have an interest in extreme sports.

- Connections: You can exclude or target individuals who are already connected to your app or Facebook page or an event you previously managed. For instance, if you plan to get to a new audience, you need to pick "Exclude people who like your page." If you want to promote a new product or offer to prior fans, choose "People who like your Facebook Page" to get to individuals who know your brand already.

Select Your Facebook Ad Placements

Scroll downward to select where the ads will show up. If you have not used Facebook advertising before, the easiest option is to utilize automatic placements. When you go with this option, Facebook automatically places your ads on various platforms. Some of these are Messenger, Instagram, and Facebook, alongside the Audience Network.

After you have garnered more experience, you may decide to choose specific locations to place your Facebook ads. Your options include the following:

- type of device

- platform type

- operating systems and mobile devices

- your budget and program

The next step is to determine the amount of cash you want to invest in your Facebook paid ads. You can set up a daily or lifetime budget. You can also plan the start and end dates if you want your ads scheduled in the future or decide to make it live instantly.

Note that running your paid ad using a schedule may be the best way of spending your ad budget. This is because you can decide to serve your ad when your target audience has more likelihood of being on Facebook. However, you will only be able to put a schedule in place if you have a lifetime budget developed for your ad.

Once you are through making selections and you are glad with the audience size indicator, select Continue.

Develop Your Ad

Here, you need to first select your ad format, then input the media and text components for your ad. The available formats will vary, depending on the campaign objectives you picked initially.

Take advantage of the preview tool beneath the page to ensure your ad looks great for all possible placements. If you are satisfied with your decisions, select the Confirm button, which is green, to submit your order. Next, wait for a Facebook email that will let you know your ad has been approved.

Using the Facebook Pixel for Ad Campaigns

Even if you are not prepared to try out some of the more complicated tactics you can implement using Facebook pixel, it is still ideal that you install it immediately. In doing so, you will have remarketing and tracking data available when you are prepared to begin optimization of your Facebook ads.

The steps below can help you set up a Facebook pixel on your website as soon as possible. First, let us take a more comprehensive look at what Facebook pixel is all about.

Facebook Pixel—What Is It?

The Facebook pixel is a little bit of code that can affect your Facebook ad campaign significantly. After placing the code on your site, it will let you monitor conversions, remarket to individuals who have previously checked out a product on your site, and develop similar audiences.

Facebook pixel functions by adding a cookie that will monitor your website visitors to enable you to contact them later on. It is also referred to as retargeting. When you advertise to individuals that have paid a visit to your site, you will be able to utilize the Facebook pixel to track the way they behave when they come back to your website. In turn, this aids you in finding out which of your adverts are more efficient while letting you target audiences that are more relevant to you.

Why You Need to Utilize a Facebook Pixel

The Facebook pixel can offer you crucial information that you can utilize in creating superior Facebook ads. It also provides you with the chance to target your audiences in a more accurate and relevant manner. When you give the pixel the chance to monitor actions that individuals take on your site after going through a Facebook ad, your ads can be developed to get to consumers that have a higher likelihood of making a conversion.

Even if you are not taking advantage of Facebook ads presently, you can still install the Facebook pixel and place it on your site. This is also applicable to Instagram ads. All you need to do is include pixel on your site before you unveil your ad on Instagram.

How does Facebook Pixel Function?

For instance, if a person clicks on your link ad and purchases one of your products after being directed to your website, the Facebook pixel will activate and report the action that has just occurred. With the help of Facebook pixel, you will be aware of when a client took action after seeing your advert on Facebook. In doing this, you will also have the capacity to get to this specific client again later with the help of a custom audience.

When the number of conversions that occur on your website keeps increasing, Facebook will automatically become better at ensuring your adverts get to individuals who have a higher probability of taking action. This is referred to as conversion optimization.

The Facebook pixel can also aid you in targeting customers that have previously displayed interest in one of your services or product by clicking an ad and checking it out. Some may probably have gone a step further by including the product in the cart before deciding to leave it and cancel the purchase.

Because the pixel is keeping track of all actions that occur on your site, you will have the capacity to easily discern the products that shoppers have found appealing. By gathering the details of visitors who have an interest in your page from your Facebook ad, you will be able to begin retargeting them efficiently.

How to Develop a Facebook Pixel

You can develop and implement the Facebook pixel via the Ads Manager following the steps below:

- Head to the pixel area.
- Select "Create a Pixel."

- Choose a name for your pixel.

- Select "Install Pixel Now."

Copy the pixel base code, then paste it between the tags on every web page, or you can paste it in the template of your site, which will let you install it on your whole website.

If you want to monitor various forms of actions of precise pages, include "events" to that precise page. The event code gives you the capacity to monitor those actions and use advertising in leveraging them.

Note that there is only a single Facebook pixel for each account. However, you can include numerous events to the pixel on various types of pages. Utilize Pixel Helper, which is a tool that aids you in authenticating your Facebook pixel. Using this tool, you can find out if your pixel is working the right way, learn to enhance performance, and troubleshoot common issues.

Facebook Pixels and Next Ad

After developing your Facebook pixel via the Ads Manager, it is now time to begin utilizing the pixel for your campaigns with the Next Ad.

When developing your campaign using the Next Ad, you will locate the Goal Specific segment underneath the Campaign Settings. This area consists of all your previously imported Facebook pixels. It also gives you access to a button that allows you to import more conversion pixels that you have developed.

Pick the pixel that you would love to utilize for your campaign. Select the type of event and choose Next. That is all. You can begin to enjoy the Facebook pixel.

Chapter 10: How to Create an LLC for Your Digital Marketing Agency Business

LLC stands for limited liability company. Creating an LLC for your digital marketing agency is the easiest method of organizing your business to safeguard your assets in the event an individual sues your business.

One or more individual can own an LLC. These individuals are called LLC members. If your LLC has a single owner, it is referred to as a single-member LLC, while that owned by more than one individual is called a multi-member LLC.

Why should you develop an LLC for your agency?

When you create an LLC for your agency, it aids in keeping you protected from lawsuits, drastically reducing your paperwork in comparison to other kinds of legal entities. Moreover, it aids in averting your agency from double taxing and aids in making your business seem more credible.

Different Kinds of LLCs

Below are a few of the most common kinds of LLCs:

- Domestic LLC: An LLC is called a domestic LLC when it carries out its business in the state where it was created. For instance, if you form the LLC for your agency in Chicago and carry out your operations there, it is a domestic LLC.

- Professional LLC: This is an LLC that is created to carry out a professional service like legal or medical practice. To develop this LLC, specific members of the LLC need to have the necessary state licenses to showcase the professional qualifications they possess.

- Foreign LLC: If your agency has an LLC and you decide to open other offices or any other form of physical presence in another state, you have to register in that state as a foreign LLC.

- Series LLC: This is a special kind of LLC where one parent LLC offers limited liability security across a series of smaller businesses. Additionally, all the smaller businesses are secured from the legal responsibilities of the others in the single series LLC.

- Presently, you will only be able to develop a series LLC in the following states: Montana, Texas, Washington DC, Minnesota, Oklahoma, Alabama, Indiana, Missouri, North Dakota, Delaware, Utah, Nevada, Illinois, Kansas, Iowa, Wisconsin, and Tennessee.

Benefits of an LLC

The following are some benefits you get from developing an LLC for your agency:

- **Protection of personal assets:** So long as there is no criminal or fraudulent behavior, LLC owners do not have personal responsibility for the lawsuits or debts of the LLC.

- **Go through taxation:** The profit of an LLC goes straight to its proprietors, who then state their part of the revenue on their personal tax returns. In essence, LLC profits get taxed just once. It is called pass-through taxation as opposed to others like a C corporation, which is liable to double taxation.

- **Easy to develop:** It is not difficult to develop an LLC for your agency. It also comes with little paperwork, which is easy to maintain as opposed to S corporations and C corporations. LLCs do not need to hold meetings annually, assign official roles, or record the resolutions and minutes of the company.

- **Enhanced credibility:** Creating an LLC for your agency aids in increasing credibility. An LLC is seen as a more professional business structure as opposed to a partnership or sole proprietorship. Adding LLC to the name of your agency allows your clients to understand that you are in serious business.

- **More business loans:** When you have developed an LLC, your agency can start to develop a credit history. It will aid your agency in gaining access to lines of credit and loans.

How to Develop an LLC for Your Agency

Forming an LLC is not as difficult as many people may believe. The steps below can make it less difficult for you:

- Select a free business name that is compliant with the LLC rules of your state.

- File formal paperwork that is known as articles of organization. After filing, pay the fee for filing, which ranges from around $100 and above, depending on the rules of your state.

- Develop an operating agreement for LLC, which lists out the duties and rights of the members of the LLC.

- Issue a notice of your intention to create an LLC. This is not a necessity in all states.

- Get permits and licenses that you may require for your agency.

Pick an LLC Name

Your LLC name has to be compliant with your LLC state's rule. These requirements may differ between states, but they are typically as follows:

- The name you choose cannot be similar to the name of an LLC filed with the LLC office.

- The name has to end with something that connotes LLC. This could be a limited company or limited liability company or an acronym of any of these.

- The name cannot consist of specific words that the state prohibits like "insurance" and "bank" among others. Note that the prohibited words differ based on specific state rules.

The office of your state's LLC can inform you how to determine if the name you have chosen is available. Most of the time, you will be able to reserve your chosen LLC name for a brief while until you have filed your article of organization. Aside from following the naming rules of the LLC in your state, you need to ensure that your name won't be a violation of the trademark of another organization.

When you have found a name that is available and legit, it is not usually essential for you to register it with the state. Your chosen business name will be registered automatically when you file your articles of organization.

File Articles of Organization

After you have decided on a name for your agency, you have to put an article of organization in place and file it with the filing office of your state's LLC. While a majority of the states utilize the term "articles of organization" when referring to the essential documents needed for developing an LLC, some states refer to it as a certificate of organization or certificate of formation.

Filing fees: You are required to pay a filing fee when turning in your articles of organization. In many states, the fees are not high and are usually not more than $100. Some other cities are more expensive. For instance, in California, there is an annual tax of $800 aside from its filing fee.

Required information: Articles of organization are brief, simple documents. You will be able to develop yours in a matter of minutes by checking the boxes and filling blanks on a form your state's filing office offers. The information you need to provide is the name of your LLC, the address, and a few times, the names of each of the owners known as members.

All owners of LLC need to put the articles in place and sign it, or they can appoint one individual to get it done.

Registered agent: You will need to list the address and name of an individual, usually one of the members of the LLC, who will function as the agent for services of process or registered agent. Your agent is the individual elected to get legal papers in the event of any lawsuit that has to do with your LLC that may come up in the future.

Develop an LLC Operating Agreement

Although it is not a necessity for you to file operating agreements with the filing office of the LLC and it is not frequently made mandatory by state law, it is crucial for you to develop one.

In the operating agreement of an LLC, you set up the rules for the operation and ownership of the business similar to corporate bylaws or a partnership agreement. An operating agreement typically consists of the following:

- interests of members in the business in percentage

- the responsibilities and rights of members

- the allocation of profit and losses

- the voting power of members

- how to manage the LLC

- the rules for taking votes and holding meetings

- buy-sell provisions, which govern what occurs if a member dies, becomes disabled, or desires to sell his or her interest.

Open a Bank Account for Your Business

To open an account for your LLC, you will require the EIN of the LLC, your articles of organization, and two means of identification. It is a crucial step to finish the process of developing a distinct financial body for your organization.

9 798457 181274